Shawn

(H) 715-327-8275
Dean (N) 715-485-9633

Living for the Moment

by

Brenda Ann Rebelein

Bloomington, IN   Milton Keynes, UK

AuthorHouse™
1663 Liberty Drive, Suite 200
Bloomington, IN 47403
www.authorhouse.com
Phone: 1-800-839-8640

AuthorHouse™ UK Ltd.
500 Avebury Boulevard
Central Milton Keynes, MK9 2BE
www.authorhouse.co.uk
Phone: 08001974150

This book is a work of non-fiction. Unless otherwise noted, the author and the publisher make no explicit guarantees as to the accuracy of

© 2006 Brenda Ann Rebelein. All rights reserved.

No part of this book may be reproduced, stored in a retrieval system, or transmitted by any means without the written permission of the author.

First published by AuthorHouse 10/24/2006

ISBN: 1-4259-5770-6 (sc)

Library of Congress Control Number: 2006908637

Printed in the United States of America
Bloomington, Indiana

This book is printed on acid-free paper.

reb@bevcomm.net

Dedication

Living for the Moment is dedicated to my mom, Marvel Mae Bartlet Niebuhr. We went on this cancer journey together, and she taught me how to live life to the fullest and how to die with courage, dignity and pride. My mom was both my hero and my friend. She will be missed, and she will never be forgotten.

Table of Contents

Acknowledgements ix

Introduction xi

Chapter 1 Getting Settled In 1

Chapter 2 Each Day is a Blessing from God 8

Chapter 3 Wishes Do Come True 27

Chapter 4 Yesterday Is Gone and Tomorrow Is Not Here,
    So Let's Enjoy Today 49

Chapter 5 God, I'm Scared 78

Chapter 6 New Beginnings For Us All 122

Chapter 7 Final Wishes and the Closing of Our Journey 153

Acknowledgements

I need to acknowledge the following people without whom Living for the Moment would have not been a success:

The amazing staff of Authorhouse. From sales to production to marketing to publicity.

Copyrighted, God's Ribbons, Message of Hope. Author Cindy Watts, for sharing your story about your own cancer journey with your mother. You gave me the courage to share my story also.

Kristine Akkermann, for helping me with my book.

Renee Burns, for stepping on board and helping out with your expertise.

The staff of Wells Library, for helping me get started and giving me encouragement to honor my mom in this wonderful book.

My husband, Mike. You're the greatest! You were my rock and a soft place to fall. Thank you for letting me leave our business to be with my mom during her cancer journey, especially the last two months. I also appreciated you doing your share of shifts taking care of mom.

My children, Monica, Lance and Josh. Thanks for being the kids a mom would always be proud of. My granddaughters, Desiree and Destiny. You always had hugs and kisses for me.

My siblings, Chuck, Bruce, Darcy and the in-laws, Thelma, Wendy and Jeremy. Mom was so proud as we all pulled together. Because of you guys, she received her wish to stay in her own home.

Grandchildren and great-grandchildren, for helping and taking care of Grandma, and for all your visits and phone calls to Grandma Marvel which helped her smile each day.

The Hospice Staff and Volunteers, for being our earth angels with all of your wonderful care. Mom's wish became a reality, and she was able to stay in her own home. It was a bond you cannot find anywhere else.

Jeanette Brandt and Mary Lou Radke, thanks for rescheduling your lives to take care of mom.

Family and friends, whether you stayed with mom or just stopped in for coffee, I will forever be grateful for you making each day a blessing and creating good times.

Dr. Mohr and the staff of the Mayo Clinic and St. Mary's in Rochester, God bless the people who care for others.

And most of all, my thanks to God, who listened to me each day. I received seven months to be with mom and to remember forever. You gave us laughter, family and friends. You helped me through those days as we were "living for the moment."

God bless each one of you. Mom is in a wonderful place. She is our guardian angel.

Introduction

This book was written at Pihls Park, about seven miles outside of Wells, Minnesota, in Faribault County, at the picnic table which was my mom's favorite place to be. I want you, my readers, to understand what kind of person our mom and grandma was before you start on our family's cancer journey with us. Mom and Dad were hard workers all their lives. They bartended together, dad worked as a plumber, and later they owned a little café. Mom decided she wanted bigger and better things, so they bought into the bar and restaurant business by the freeway and named it Club 90. It was their life and ours, too, as we kids worked there. My brother, Chuck, and his wife Thelma were part owners for a few years. Dad got sick at the early age of 55, and he passed away when he was 65. Mom continued the restaurant business for a few more years, but over time, it became too much for her, so she went into retirement for a few months. Not long after, she was back working for restaurants. She was happiest in the kitchen and dealing with people. When Mom's legs got bad, it forced her into retirement. Now what would she do? She cooked for all of her family and friends, which included cooking for my brother, Bruce, and his employees twice a week.

Mom and Dad built the house in which they lived for many years. They built it by the lake, and Mom loved to watch the geese fly in and out. It was a big part of her day. One thing we all knew for certain is that Mom loved us very much. She had a way of walking into a crowded room and brightening it with her smile and her great disposition. Mom never judged any of us. She always seemed to show us the way when a situation was just too hard to understand. It was fun to stop in at her house just to talk. Mom always enjoyed life. Just being around her made you feel good because she was so full of life and always enjoying a good time.

Each grandchild and great-grandchild had a special bond with her from their day of birth. That bond grew stronger through the years, and they became close pals. When the grandchildren did something naughty or were acting up, all Grandma had to do was give them the look. She loved taking the kids camping or fixing them a meal after

xi

they had gone swimming or finished with school activies. We all have fond memories of our mom and grandma which we will keep in our hearts forever.

We had many camping trips, good times at the casinos, and trips to LasVegas. On her last trip to Las Vegas with Darcy and Jeremy, she won a thousand dollars. She called my brother, Chuck, at two in the morning to tell him the good news (I'm glad she had his number). Mom loved Circus Circus in Las Vegas and the carousel. And aside from Las Vegas, she loved reading romance books and catching bullheads. She would fry them to a crisp, and she taught all of the grandchildren to love them too. One time I like to remember is when Mom and Dad were coming home from a vacation in the motorhome. Mom was driving, and Dad was sleeping. Dad woke up by the lake in Waterville to find Mom fishing, and he saw that she had already filled half of a bucket with bullheads.

Mom also loved watching and talking about politics. She got that from her dad. It was an interest she shared with him, and she loved a good debate. Mom was a happy, outgoing person who loved laughter as much as life. Even knowing that cancer would take her life, Mom told us that each day was a blessing because she knew her family's love would last forever. When Mom received the news, she was concerned about the people she loved, including Dr. Mohr who was her doctor for twenty years. Mom put people first and her cancer second.

God works through people, as I saw with my mom. A few months before her results came back, Mom had her basement cleaned out and took care of things that she had put off. It seemed as if, in the back of her mind, she knew something was wrong. I had always liked a certain Christmas snowball, and she gave it to me out of the blue, even though it was a joke between us that she was going to will it to me. She had a cat named Kitty Kat, and she had him put to sleep. It was the only cat my mom would take in because she hated cats when she was growing up. A few years prior, on Christmas Day, Mom found Kitty Kat, who was three-legged, blind and deaf, out on her deck. Mom took him in and loved him dearly, and when she put him to sleep, she said that she was the only one who could love him. It was sudden and hard to understand. Things just did not add up. Mom knew something was going on. Mom had flu like symptoms. Darcy and I were taking her to the Mayo Clinic for testing.

On September 1, 2004, I got a call from Darcy around 9 p.m. saying she and Mom were back from Mom's second visit to the Mayo Clinic in two days. They had been running tests, and the results were in. "Come over. We need to talk," she said. I prayed the whole way over there for guidance. Everyone else lives in town or close by, but I had to drive seven miles to get there. I could feel the tension and see it on everyone's faces. I'll never forget how my sister looked. You could tell she had been crying, but she was trying to look so strong. And Mom, she'd always been so classy, always tried to look her best, but at the moment it was like you could actually see her age. She told me to take a seat.

"Kids, its not good," she said. "I have cancer. They are not giving me much time. There will be no tears, as I have had a good life. There is nothing to feel bad about. There are three things that I want to do yet before I get too sick: one, go to a casino and win a good pot; two, have a big party one more time; and three, I want to go camping one more time. And this weekend, three of my family members I hear is going camping, and I don't know whose camper we will be in, but I'm going camping. That is all I have to say."

It was like I was hit by a ton of bricks. *Okay God, I thought, You have changed my plans. I had thought Mom would be here forever. She is only seventy-six. But I will not ask why because it is not for me to judge. I just need to know where we go from here. And I will need your help as this is too big for me to do alone.* I looked at my siblings and then at Mom and said, "Yes, Mom, you received the news, and if you say no tears, we will follow with you. If you can be strong, we will be too." The rest of the night was a blur. We talked some more, but it was like we were in a foreign country and didn't understand what was being said. She wanted to be alone that night, and we wanted someone to stay. But she reminded us that there would be plenty of nights to come when she would need someone to stay.

When I got home, I had to tell my kids. It was already written on my face. We told Josh who still lives at home, and we called Monica and Lance who are older and have their own apartments. They wanted to know right away, over the phone, because they could tell in our voices that something was going on. I told them we just have to stick

xiii

together and be strong. We cried and tried to remember what we have to be grateful for. I needed one night to get a hold of myself. We were losing a woman we all looked up to as she was being called home soon by our higher power.

Dr. Mohr, Mom's doctor for 20 years, explained to us that with pancreatic cancer, she only had a few months to live. He said it was a place that couldn't be reached and was thus inoperable. We just needed to enjoy the time she had left. He did recommend a stomach bypass to help her take in nutrition. She had already lost 39 lbs., and he wanted her to check into the hospital immediately to regain some weight before surgery. It was like a weight had been lifted from Mom's shoulders. All this time, she had been smiling and smiling to cover up her fear. All her life, she had always been the responsible one, the one in control, but now she could finally let go and follow doctor's orders. Surgery went well, and we hoped for at least six to eighteen months with her. We mostly hoped for one more Christmas.

Mom took the whole thing in stride. One day, her high school friend called the hospital. She was in tears and had just heard the news. Mom reassured her. "I'm going to a better place," she said. "I will be with Marvin. In fact, I can't wait. Be happy for me. I tell you what, you have a good cry and then call me back. You'll feel better." A few minutes later, her friend called back, and they were able to talk about the good times.

Mom stayed in the hospital until September 15th, and then we contacted Crossroads Community Hospice Program. My brother Bruce met Hospice at Mom's house and got things rearranged according to code. They helped us with her medication, taught us how to care for her, and generally took over her little 8 foot by 10 foot room which would eventually come to mean so much to us. Words cannot express how grateful we are to them. They really walked us through the whole journey which was all new to us, and they gave us the opportunity to keep Mom at home. It was her wish to pass away there, and it was a promise we had to try to keep.

We set up the schedules for 24-hour care, bathing, medication, etc. I took medical leave from my job and from my responsibilities to Mike and our handyman business. God really gave me the time to be with Mom. One night, she even managed to join the family, all big campers,

xiv

for dinner on one of our big family camping trips. Just about everyone was there, and we all knew it was the last time Mom would be sitting by a campfire. You could see how much she was enjoying herself. Mom even said the food was good, which is a big compliment coming from such a great cook. The whole night was full of the kind of memories that last a lifetime. Mom cooked on the days she could.

Mom was always in control, like I said. She planned her own funeral because she didn't want us to mess it up and so she'd get exactly what she wanted. She planned the music and to have Barb sing, she planned the poems she wanted people to hear, and she planned the menu—her BBQ pork sandwiches with her special BBQ sauce. Barb a friend is singing for her funeral, made a tape of mom's favorite songs. One night, she went off to be by herself and then called me into her room later to tell me she had picked the day of her death. You'll have to keep reading to find out if she was right, but the point is just that she was that kind of lady.

Those first two months were exhausting as we all got used to the new routines and the new complications to our lives. But we settled into it, and we learned to take those good moments and savor them for all they're worth. Because it was so hectic, my notes from that time are scattered, but by the third month, I was keeping almost daily journal entries. There are also a few poems and a lot of prayers, all of which helped me along the way.

Mom was an upbeat, positive, kind-hearted woman. Since Mom worked with the public for so many years, she received many cards each day through her journey. It showed how well she was liked. Mom was good to her family and friends, and I feel that God planned her cancer journey so that she would have time to get things in order, to be with her family and friends, and to have a perfect good-bye. I wrote *Living for the Moment* in honor of her. She wanted us to remember her as she had lived; and, closer to the end, she wanted to help me know that life is about helping people. I took our cancer journey and put it into words. When you love someone, you always remember them as they were. The hard part for me was sharing the bad days, but they were only moments. I will always remember Mom for her smiling face and for her humor which went so far. We truly did have the perfect good-bye.

Our Family Tree

Marvin & Marvel.

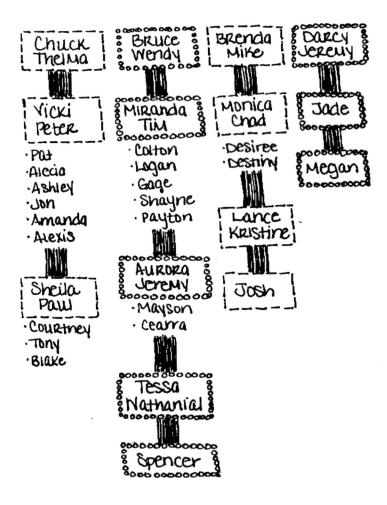

MADE BY:
Courtney O'Byrne

Chapter 1

Getting Settled In

October 2004

We are now in our second month on this cancer journey, and we are all getting tired. We have had to reschedule our lives and make time for our shifts to do our share. Family and friends are helping with the shifts. I can not think with how tired I'm getting. I work with Mike all day and stay with mom at night and go back to work in the morning. I just need to keep focused. I do not sleep well at night because I think she may call me to help her with going to the bathroom. Mom tries to go to the bathroom alone, but it is hard for her to walk and, we are afraid she will fall.

Mom is doing great emotionally. She is always in a good mood and happy to see us when we start our shift. Mom has to be scared, but she does not show it. I have asked God to give me strength.

Mom is starting to pass out things that she has promised people for years. These are things she wants handed down or things that people have given her that they will get back. Mom and I have had this joke going for years. Since I was in school, she has had these five ugly pictures that are a set, and I have wanted her to get rid of them and put something new up. Mom has willed them to me and expects them to be on my wall in my living room. Mom has loved them for years. I think my wanting Mom to replace them made her love them even more. Mom is asking her children, grandchildren, family and friends what they want for keepsakes. It is hard for people to understand. They are trying to get over the shock that Mom has cancer as she has been so healthy and this has taken her down so fast. People come to see her, and she is giving her things away.

And she's in a good mood considering what is going on in her life. Mom is cheering her company up. It's like Mom says, "If you don't say what you want, then don't complain later when you don't get it." When her best friend from high school stopped by for a visit, she asked Mom

1

if they could have their picture taken together. Mom hates having her picture taken. She wanted to fix her hair, do her makeup, and change clothes. Mom came out in her blue dress, and as they posed, just before the picture was snapped, she flashed her friend! You can imagine her shock, but Mom knew her friend was having a hard time dealing with the news of Mom's cancer. She was willing to do anything to help her, and she thought this would make the picture even more memorable. Whenever someone came over struggling with Mom's future, by the time they left, Mom had let them know she was ready to die. She wanted us all to be happy for her. Plus, Mom said that if she couldn't laugh and have fun, she might as well die. When her niece from California came to visit, she also wanted a picture with her Auntie Marvel in the blue dress. She had flown home to see Mom as soon as she heard the news. They were close, and she had worked in the restaurant with Mom. So when she asked for a picture, Auntie Marvel flashed her as well.

Chuck and I brought mom a gift for when she needs us. Chuck brought her a bike horn. I brought her a bell we use in the restaurant. She is having fun with them.

Hospice is teaching us what we are supposed to be doing. The big thing is learning the medication. We are not in the medical field, and they are leaving us in charge. Mom sure laughs about that. It is all in black and white, and they have made it easy for us. The bath time and pill time are on a schedule. The nurse comes and checks in. She sees how things are going and if we have any questions, and let me tell you, there are days we have a lot of them, but she answers them all. We are marking down any info that should be recorded.

Mom is eating well. She teases us that she can eat whatever she wants and she does not have to watch her weight like we do. The hospice staff is so wonderful to us. They are on call twenty-four hours a day. They never lose their patience with us as they go from house to house dealing with death each day. God bless them all. And I know they must be asked at each house, "How much longer does our loved one have left?" They say each patient is different, and the time they guess they could be wrong. We just need to enjoy today.

When the hospice staff comes to Mom's house, she makes them feel so welcome. She is getting to know them on a personal note and

Living for the Moment

learning about their lives outside of work. Mom always wants them to be treated with coffee and treats and for them to leave with a smile.

Mom is getting a bath once a week. We have another blessing. Mom's main bath lady will be a family friend. Mom is so tickled about it. They talk the whole time about the good old days. Mom has always told us how good she was through the years, but their stories are saying something different.

Mom has always been a gal who thinks appearance is a big thing. Mom does not leave the house without her hair and makeup looking nice, making sure everything is in place. Now that she is staying in her home and not going out, it is the same way. When she wakes up, she makes a shot to the bathroom to get cleaned up and to get her hair done and do her face. Mom loves having her hair done every other week. Mom tried to go to the beauty shop, but she just could not do it. Candy, Mom's hairdresser, called, and she will come and do Mom's hair every other Monday because that is her day off. This is another example of how, if you are good to people, what goes around comes around. Mom loves cooking for Candy. They have a good buddy system going. Candy just has to remember to bring enough hair spray. Mom loves hair spray. So Mom is on her little stool waiting for Candy and her bath is already done.

Mom has us caretakers working our shifts. Anyone who comes and visits gets a good meal or something to go with coffee. No one leaves unfed. She will say, "What are you serving if anyone stops in?" This is something we have all talked about. Mom's life has been cooking, but, in the end, they told us there will come a time when it will be hard for her to swallow.

Clothes are starting to make Mom uncomfortable. She asked me if it would be wrong if she wore nice nightgowns or two-piece sleepwear outfits with a nice robe. We all told her she needs to be comfortable. Now when the family stops in for a visit, she tells them to bring her some new sleepwear next time they come so she can look nice. Leave it to our Mom to be so bold.

It is nothing for Mom to have five or more visitors a day. I asked her if she was getting sick of company, but Mom replied, "People have been my whole life. Do not take my company away. There will be a day when I will feel I do not have much time left. My appearance will be getting

Brenda Ann Rebelein

bad. When I say no company, please promise me this. I want people to remember me the way I was because this could get rough. The only ones I want to see me are my four kids." Mom looked me right in the eye, and right then I knew it was a promise I would keep. This is Mom's life, and she should have the right to be respected in her wishes.

Mom has always been the life of the party, and she loves to play jokes. She loves to make people laugh. When Mom was healthy, she liked to have a berry wine cooler once in awhile. Mom is really starting to lose weight even though she is eating, so I got her favorite wineglass out and put an Ensure in it and told her it was a berry wine cooler. She drank some and said, "This is good wine." Then she looked at me and said, "You fool. This is that chalk stuff you have me drinking to gain weight." We got a good laugh out of it, and she kept drinking. Later that night she told me how she misses being in her sunken living room with a fireplace. I asked her, "Why don't you go in there?"

"Everyone one is afraid I will fall," she said. There are four steps to go down, and Mom is not very stable on her feet.

"Let's go, and if you fall, I will just pick you up," I said. Mom had this big smile on her face.

"Okay, lets go." She was so happy to be in her living room. She just kept looking around like she was seeing it for the first time.

Mom loves reading her daily paper each day. She asked me to go get it even though she had already read it. The cancer is taking over, and she's been falling asleep because of her medications. The paper kept falling because she can not stay awake. I was having second thoughts about whether or not I should have let her go down there. But then she jumped awake. "This is dumb," she laughed. "We need something to wake us up. Go get the phone." It was 9:00 p.m., and she called my brother Chuck and told him that she was craving potato chips and needed some right away. She chuckled and hung up.

"Why did you do that?" I asked.

She replied, "I'm testing his love. We will see if he passes." Five minutes later, here came Chuck's daughter Sheila who lives next door with two kinds of potato chips. Mom laughed and said, "Chuck did not pass the test. I'm tired now. Will you two help me to bed?" With Mom, nothing surprises us any more. This is our Mom and Grandma. She will have humor until the day she dies.

Living for the Moment

A couple of nights later, Mom was getting settled down in bed around 8:00 at night. I had her tucked in bed for the night. She knows that I'm a push over and will do as I'm told. She was lying in bed and asked me to open the closet door and hand her that file cabinet. It is one of those closet doors you just want to hurry and close. Soon Mom asked me to hand her this box and then another box, and she was quickly going through them and pushing them to the side. Then she said to start a pile to throw away and then another pile to keep so someone could have it or sell it. Before I knew it, we had a mess, as this bedroom is only 8 feet by 10 feet. She had me moving so fast I did not have time to think. It was hard to even move around in there. Mom's bed was piled high with old coats, and we found her fur coat. She talked about how many of her granddaughters had used it for prom or other events. She wants to hand it down to Darcy or me. Soon I had the hallway full, and my piles were getting higher. We got everything cleaned out, and she was happy because that was one thing she wanted to do while she still could—clean out her closets and drawers. Then she said, "Look, it is 11:00. Please clean off my bed and shut the door. I have cancer you know, and I need my sleep." We both ended up laughing at the mess I had yet to clean up. I got everything into the hall and shut her door. I could hear her giggling in her room as I was putting things in their place. It may have been a lot of work for me, but she enjoyed herself looking at things she had not seen for years. She liked going through a box that had old articles she had put in the paper about the restaurant that she owned for twenty years. It was fun to laugh and get away from the cancer that has been controlling all of our lives.

Lance and Kristine stopped in to see Mom the other day. They had a surprise for her… their engagement! Lance bought a beautiful ring and surprised Kristine with it. Mom and I both had tears in our eyes. We always hoped Lance would find a good mate, and he has. Mom told them she wouldn't be there for the wedding, but she would be smiling down from above. "Always have good communication, and have fun together. Don't let things bother you," she told them. They spent the rest of the day with her.

Mom was getting ready for bed one night and she was staring out in the dark for a long time. I asked her, "What are you looking at out there?"

Brenda Ann Rebelein

"Do you think my grandchildren know how much I love them?" she asked.

"Yes, they do, Mom, because they love you just the same," I replied.

Some nights Mom sleeps peacefully, and others she is restless. My journal is going to help me on the good and bad days of this cancer journey. I will write on the times when I feel that my emotions need to be heard.

Tonight, right before Darcy and Jeremy closed the meat market. Mom called and put in a big order for the next time Darcy comes to stay the night at Mom's. I did not know what Mom was up to. With her, you never know. When she was cleaning her drawers out, she found a fifteen-year-old gift certificate for the meat market that Darcy and Jeremy bought from the previous owner. The gift certificate was outdated and not issued by valid owners, but she was going to use this certificate for the food she just ordered. She was laughing so hard about pulling the wool over their eyes. "You cannot use that. It is not good," I explained to her.

"Watch me," she laughed. When Darcy came to deliver the food, she was shocked how Mom had planned to pay for her order. It made for an interesting night.

Sheila thinks Tony sprain his finger Mom told her to go get him. She had me unthaw some ice cream so we could have the sticks. She made a splinter with duct tape for Tony's finger She talked with Tony the whole time she was working on his finger I had tears in my eyes when I seen mom helping Tony. I think of all the times mom is helping her grandchldren.

Things are more organized with our schedule. We are learning the medications, and hospice is being so patient with us. Mary Lou, Mom's sister, was staying with her until 5:00. Mom told Mary Lou that she thought there was something wrong with her body, things felt funny, and to call her kids home. She felt she was dying. She wanted Pastor Soli called. We received the call from Bruce to come home. We did not know what was happening to Mom. I knew in my heart that it was going to get a lot worse than this when it is her time to pass away. We arrived at Mom's. Chuck and his wife, Thelma; Darcy and her husband, Jeremy; Bruce and his wife, Wendy; my husband Mike and myself were all there.

Living for the Moment

Bruce called hospice. They would be a call away for any questions we had. They reassured us that Mom was not passing away. Mom was so tired that it was hard for her to keep her eyes open. She wanted to speak to us kids alone. She spoke to us about making the most out of our lives, how sad she was not to see the grandchildren grow up, and how she would watch from heaven up above. She said she loved us all. She asked us to share anything we had to add to the conversation. It was hard for Mom to stay awake. We told her we loved her and we would not leave her. We would always be okay. We had a great life together. Pastor Soli arrived. Mom insisted that she was passing away that night. No one was telling her any different. We all gathered around Mom's bed. We took turns going in Mom's room to be with her. She could not stay awake to talk to us. We had communion with Mom. Then she heard no one had supper yet, so we sent for chicken to be deliver to Mom's house. We ate as a family and then went home.

One day, I went to Mom's for my shift, and she was sitting at the table looking serious and sitting up tall like she meant business. She said, "Today is the day." I knew right away what she meant. Years ago, she bought herself a new ring when her wedding ring was stolen. She had planned for the ring to go to me at the time of her death. I will hand it down to Jade, and then it will pass through each generation of girls and between Darcy's girls and mine. I looked at Mom in disbelief. I did not want this day to be now. I was not ready, but Mom looked at me and said, "Stop it. I have lost too much weight. I do not want to loose this ring. I want the joy of seeing it on your finger while I'm still enjoying life. So here, put it on. Enjoy it as much as I did. I know you'll keep it cleaner." She giggled, and I received my new ring with pride.

Chapter 2

Each Day is a Blessing from God

November 2004

We are now facing our third month of this cancer journey. I really need to slow things down. It is so hard not being able to say how much longer we have and what will happen in the future. I need to have faith. I know we will be taken care of because God watches us each day. It's hard just knowing that Mom's life here on earth is growing shorter. Ever since I was young, I have always had a journal for writing my feelings down. It's a good place to go when there's a lot on my mind. I can get my feelings out and move on, and I have a lot to get rid of since I have been putting my emotions on the back burner. I work with Mike in our business, take care of my family, and now take care of Mom! My main goal is to be with her every day, as we do not know how much time she has left. I have been signing up to stay with Mom for all of the shifts that I can, always trying to work around the business. Family and friends are helping us.

We got a good laugh the other day as we were setting up the schedule for this month. Little four year-old Blake, Sheila and Paul's boy, was at great-grandma's house. As we were putting our names down, Blake was walking around and around the dining room table. Finally, someone asked him what was wrong. "Everyone gets a shift. I want my name on a day," he said. The laughter and the smile that lifted Mom's face was priceless.

"Well, get signed up," Mom told him. Blake was proud that he could do his share.

I'm going to start a daily journal as things are changing in our lives. It's a place for me to find comfort and write. Mom has changed since last month—she's so much weaker, and she's in a wheelchair when needed. Her cancer is taking over, and she's only eating bites of food now. Sometimes, she will be hungry for something, but by the time we get it to her, she can't eat it. She never drank Coke before, and now we can't keep enough of it in the house. She is so thirsty all the time.

Living for the Moment

She's also getting confused at times. We take it one day at a time, and some days I even have to slow that down. I think this is a scary time because we've never been through this. Dad was in the hospital a lot the last five years of his life. He passed away in the Vets Hospital, and we didn't have any of this caretaking to do. I'm amazed how we have pulled together as a family and amazed at all the friends that came to take care of our loved one, Marvel Mae. Mom has always been there for us, and now it is time for us to be there for her. The names are too numerous to begin to mention how they have helped us make this journey so much easier. I pray that I can repay them all some day. God bless them all.

Sunday, November 7, 2004

Bruce and Wendy's daughter, Tessa, stopped by to see Grandma on her way back to school. She will be graduating soon from St. Thomas in Minneapolis. Mom has been her biggest supporter to keep her going forward in her schooling and to get her teaching degree. Tessa and Mom had some time alone this afternoon. Tessa has found her true love. She knows that Nathaniel is her soul mate. They are now enaged. It's hard knowing that Mom will not be at the wedding in person, but as she says, "You wait your whole life for your dream wedding. I will be there in spirit. I would not expect those kids to throw a wedding together just so I could be there. No, this is their day. They should plan it for themselves, and I will watch over to see that it's done right." Mom, of course, just smiled as they spent the afternoon together.

Tonight, Mom was leaving the bathroom after flushing the toilet when it started overflowing with clear water. I grabbed the plunger and started plunging as fast as I could. Mom was watching me and laughing. Thank God, it was clear water. Mom, a plumber's wife for so many years, pushed me aside. "Give me that," she said. "You plunge like an old lady makes love. Go get me some hot water from the kitchen. I mean hot as you can get. Hurry." She worked on the toilet as a full stream of water poured over the edge.

"We're working on a toilet," I said. "Not delivering babies." But she gave me her "hurry up" look, so I went to get the water. When I poured the hot water in the toilet, the flow subsided quickly. Dad would have been proud.

Brenda Ann Rebelein

There were at least three inches of water in the hallway and bathroom, and Mom looked down at the mess as she cleaned herself up. "Looks like you have a mess to clean up," she said. "I don't know if you heard, but I have cancer. I need my sleep." She smiled, and off to bed she went. I could hear her giggling when she got to the bedroom because she had to ask for my help.

Monday, November 8, 2004

I'm on my third shift in a row of staying with mom. Our shifts are running from 8 a.m. to 5 p.m. and 5 p.m. to 8 a.m. Mom is very restless today. We have medication in case she gets restless, and now we need to give it to her. Mom has been able to cook up until now, but, as I say, things are changing. She almost burned herself, and then she wanted to work with the knives. I knew I had to do something. I held the medication in my hands twice while she was cooking but couldn't give it to her. Mom would have fallen three times if I had not been there to catch her. She's getting a lot weaker each day. I prayed so hard to God to help! The third time I went for the medication, I felt God carry me to the pill container.

After a few minutes, she started to relax and thought she should go sit down and rest for a minute, leaving her cooking behind. I talked her into a nap by telling her that I was sure tired, and if she would rest then so would I. Mom thought it was best if I got some much-needed rest. Once she was safe in bed, I had my time to rest and think. Why couldn't I give Mom her medication? I can face that she's dying, but my emotions keep changing. I can face that she is not herself anymore, but I don't want to play a part in keeping her in bed. I think today was a learning lesson for me. If I plan on taking care of Mom, I have to keep her out of harm's way. I need to keep her safe. It is time for me to step up to the plate and do what is best for Mom, not me. We have had our good times here since she came home from the hospital, whether we were alone or with her company.

The hospice aide gives mom a bath a couple of times per week. One day, after her bath, she was so cold, and I could not warm her up. Then she thought of her fur coat and had me get it for her. She was sitting there praying someone would come and visit. She always has company here, but the moment she wants someone to come, no one is

10

Living for the Moment

here. She had her hair done, wore fresh makeup, and was sitting in her chair with her fur coat on. With a big smile on her face, she said, "Do I look like a dying woman?"

"No, Mom," I replied. "You look like you are ready to take on the world." Mom ended up falling asleep in her fur coat. But it is time to face the facts. She's dying. I didn't want her to get cancer, I didn't give her cancer, and she didn't want this for herself. She needs to be my patient when I'm taking care of her. What is best for my patient? I need to ask myself that whenever I get into tough situations. I will keep this attitude until the day she passes away. I need to listen to the hospice nurse and learn and tell myself that I'm doing okay.

We have never been an arguing family. Mom always says, "Do not fight." But then here she goes, doing things and blaming someone else. Then she just sits back and laughs. When I asked her why, she said that she's dying and wants to liven up the place. One time, she accused Chuck of not emptying the commode while he was caring for her on one of his shifts, so I checked and called Chuck. When I got him on the phone, I told him that his clean-ups would be checked before he went home from now on. He promised me Mom had not used the commode, but it looked like she had. When Mom started laughing, I knew what she had done. She had added water and toilet paper to the commode so Chuck would get in trouble. Yes, I had to apologize to my brother, and Mom has been doing little things like that ever since we brought her home. She says that if we laugh and have fun, it will keep us happy because there is nothing to be sad about.

There are some days and nights when I will not write exactly how things went. There were nights we talked about what the future will be like without her in it, and how she wants everyone to be happy and stay strong. The Christmas gifts she found in the closet the night we cleaned will go to my siblings. Of course she would want to get the last laugh, and these are joke gifts. I never dreamed how close cancer could bring a family together the way it did for ours, but my days and nights with mom are mine alone, and I do not have to share them with anyone.

Tuesday, November 9, 2004

I am going to Mom's tonight for the night shift. We are all getting tired emotionally and physically. Yesterday was a good lesson for me.

11

Brenda Ann Rebelein

I will not be afraid to give Mom a certain medication if needed. She is weak, and though her mind is telling her she can go, her body is not keeping up. She is short-tempered one minute and laughing the next. This is the Mom and Grandma we love. These are just not the actions we know, and this is all starting to show in our own families as we take care of Mom around the clock. Our families miss us, and yet we all know we need to do this for Grandma. I tell my family that we need the strength to move on, and we will not lose our faith as God is taking care of us.

Tonight was terrible. Mom was restless and testy. At 7:30 she went downstairs to the basement to clean and sort through things. She wouldn't take any medication for me and kept pushing it away. She knew it would make her sleepy, and she had work to do. Mom has so much unknown strength in her upper body. Where did it come from? She was picking up boxes and moving things around. Her legs are weak, though, so she would stay in one place. At one point, a bed mattress started to fall, and I was afraid it would fall on her, so I moved quickly and hurt my back. When she was finally satisfied with what she had done, we went back up stairs.

This is not Mom, so it is hard to see her this way. My back is hurting. I pulled a muscle, I'm sure. Mom finally took her medication and then went into the bathroom for an hour to do her hair, clean her face, and get ready for bed. She has always loved being in front of the mirror. She was winking at me and telling me that she loved me and not to be mad or sad. She knew I was upset, but still she couldn't understand what was going on. Bedtime and medication time was a blessing. One positive thing is that Mom is good about taking her medication in the morning and at bedtime. I'm tired and will feel better once I have some sleep. I love my mom so much. The cancer is taking my mom away, but our love for her will always stay.

Wednesday, November 10, 2004

I did not go to Mom's today. I need a day for my family and to be away from the situation. It is so good to be home. I miss my home and family. Mom was back to normal again today, like nothing had happened. I called her twice, once to wish her good morning and then

Living for the Moment

again to wish her good night as I have always done, even before she got sick.

Thursday, November 11, 2004

I have another day off from Mom's. My back is a little sore yet. Mom is very weak. Her feet are swollen and blue, and she can't walk. The hospice nurse is coming. We now have Mom in Depends. They will be changing her medication again and adding more medication. But right now, I have some family time for me.

Friday, November 12, 2004

I work the night shift at Mom's. She is still very weak. She can't walk and is very confused. In a way, it is a blessing she can not walk. I'm afraid she will break a hip. Mom took her medication well for me today, and things went well tonight. One minute, Mom is confused, and the next, she is back to being Mom. But tonight she was making jokes. She found some loose pills and wanted to know which one of us was not doing our job. They were pills she had before hospice came in our lives. She even made jokes about dying. We spent the night in her bedroom since she couldn't walk and was comfortable in bed. She would be talking about things she planned to do or where she wanted to go, and she would forget that she's dying. Then she would remember, and she'd laugh and say, "For dumb, I won't be here." I think Mom will keep her humor until she dies. She's on oxygen at nighttime now. I'm afraid of it. I know it sounds dumb. I don't know why I'm afraid of it. Mom actually grabbed me and told me to just try it, and then she pulled me onto the bed with her and tried putting that oxygen hose up my nose. We laid in that bed, laughing. Just for a moment, the cancer was gone. Mom was proud that she could still take me on. It's hard to think of my days without this wonderful lady.

Saturday, November 13, 2004

We had two hospice volunteers to take care of Mom today. We just had to do something because we all have jobs, and we are running out of people to stay with her. We're also tired from working full-time and staying with Mom. Chuck is a truck driver, and Bruce, Darcy and I all have our own businesses. Bruce helps during the day, Chuck and Darcy

13

Brenda Ann Rebelein

are staying at night. Grandkids are helping us. The hospice volunteers will stay a few hours at a time. We worked, and then we went out for lunch with my family. I tried to leave the situation with Mom behind me for just a little while.

I had to stay with Mom for a few hours this afternoon, and her little house was full of grandchildren and great grandchildren. Mom is proud when the house is full of kids. Mom wanted me to do tricks for the kids, and she told me I should do as I'm told since she is my mother. She had the kids all laughing. They all had a good afternoon. Later, Mom took a nap in her wheelchair, and she looked comfortable and content. She would wake up and enjoy watching the geese on the lake. Pastor Peter Soli came and saw Mom. She did not say too much, not as much as she usually talks while he is here. When he was getting ready to leave, he started the Lord's Prayer, and Mom sat up nice and tall and said the Lord's Prayer with us. Prayers help us all right now. Mom's body is really swollen, and she's telling us, "I can't eat any more, I can't go in the basement again, and this is the week I can't walk any more." We will wait and see where we go from here and take it as it comes. Mom has accepted everything that's been handed to her with such grace. I can learn a lot from her.

Sunday, November 14, 2004

It's Sunday today, and it's my double-shift day. Mom got up once to use the bathroom, and she has slept all day. It is hard seeing her just lying there so peacefully. We have two good months to cherish. This little house has never been so full with family and friends. We are always having a good time here. How I wish she would jump up and cook a good meal for someone—that's always what she was doing before she got sick. She loved being in the kitchen, cooking or making flower arrangements. She made one flower arrangement while she and Dad were on a vacation. I promised her she'd always have pretty flowers on her grave.

When Mom woke up she couldn't walk or stand on her feet as they are so swollen. Thank God, Mike and Josh stopped by to see how things were going. Mike helped me since Mom can not do anything for herself anymore. It was like she was dead weight. Mike used to work in a nursing home before we started our business, so he has this

Living for the Moment

background and knows how to handle people in need. Mom had her grandkids here, and it distracted her from thinking about not being able to walk. She was busy playing with the little ones. Miranda, Bruce's daughter, was here with her kids, Logan, Gage and Shayna.

Later in the afternoon she slept, but she cried in her sleep. She was calling for her mom and dad. Mom has been talking very emotionally in her sleep. She talks about how she wants to die and why God is not coming for her. She's awake one minute, and then the next she's chatty but with her eyes closed. I could not keep her in bed. She kept wanting to walk. I kept giving her medication for restlessness. She's is fighting so hard to die tonight. She keeps asking me, "Is it okay if I die on your shift?" I let her know that I would be next to her with all my other siblings. She would talk out of her head one minute, and then the next she was holding a conversation I could understand. She said she was going to go to college and be a doctor. She wanted to know if I thought she could do it. I told her, "You can do anything you want once you have your mind made up."

Mom was sitting on the side of her bed, crying for her mom and dad. They keep calling her name. I told her that they want her to come with them, but God does not have her room ready yet, so we have to wait. Mom and I prayed together. She folded her hands tight across her chest and kept repeating, "Let me go tomorrow. Let me go tomorrow." Finally, Mom settled down. She did not try to get out of bed all night. It gives me peace of mind to sleep next to her at night.

Monday, November 15, 2004

Mom woke up and was crying a lot and rocking back and forth. She does not want to face the fact that she can't walk. We had problems with Mom taking her pills this morning. Mary Lou, Mom's sister, is here to take care of Mom for the day. I put the pills in vanilla pudding and then she didn't know she had taken her medication. Hospice told me to do that. We got Mom to the commode, as it is still hard for her to walk because her feet are so swollen. It was hard for her to comprehend what she was doing and how to do it. Mom is still doing a lot of talking to her mom and dad and her husband Marvin who are all in heaven waiting for her. She is having little conversations with us. My shift is done, and it is so hard to leave her and go to work. She cried in my arms as I held

15

Brenda Ann Rebelein

her. It made me want to crawl in bed with her and let her know that it's okay. We called for reinforcements which were the grandchildren and great-grandchildren. The minute they walk in, she calms down. The grandchildren have been Mom's world. Darcy, Jade and Megan stayed the night tonight, and she was a lot chattier because of it. She was in a good mood but very confused. She cried all night.

Tuesday, November 16, 2004

Mom woke up weepy this morning. She slept a lot today. When she got up, she asked, "What's wrong with me?"

I told her, "Mom you have cancer." She closed her eyes and paused for a minute.

"I know we will get in the car and go to Rochester and go to the Mayo Clinic and see Dr. Mohr in the Baldwin Building, 4th floor, and he will tell me what's wrong with me."

Mom then drifted back to sleep. Since she has become so restless, we put a recliner next to her bed. I have been sleeping there so if she wakes up in the middle of the night and tries to get out of bed, then I will wake up. I want mom to know someone is close to her as she sleeps. Mom woke up a couple of times in the middle of the night. She said she had been in hell and did not want to be there. She told me she had to prove that she deserves to be in heaven. Mom wanted me to call hospice and tell them it will not be much longer. I feel for the hospice staff nurses that get calls all hours of the night. It takes those special people to deal with death every day. She asked me if she could die on my shift, and I told her that I would be honored.

Wednesday, November 17, 2004

Mom has gotten up four times since 4:00 a.m. She is so confused, and she's crying. She doesn't understand why all the people are coming to her house when she lives alone. Mom wanted me to go get Tony, Sheila's son who lives next door, so we could take him to the show. This was at 7:00 a.m. She got so mad at me because I wouldn't take her. She rolled away from me and told me to leave her alone. Then she slept for awhile. This is getting harder as I watch Mom slip away and become someone I do not know. I will tell her I need her to go to heaven and

Living for the Moment

get things ready for me. I know how they need to know that the loved ones they leave behind will be okay. It is not in our hands of course.

Mom was restless again this morning, and she was talking about being in hell and how scared she was. Mom is crying a lot today. She thinks the world of the hospice nurses, and she wants them to come and live with her so she can cook for them everyday. Mom loves the new underpants the hospice staff brought her. They are called Depends. Mom is a lot weaker and holding little conversation with us. Bruce was with her tonight and she had half of a cinnamon roll that she imagined was made by a friend who passed away many years ago. Mom was in her wheelchair and wanted to go and see if the cemetery looks good and ready for her when she passes away. She wanted Bruce to walk her there. He walked around Mom's small house for thirty minutes, and she was happy he had done that for her. She thought it looked nice. The rest of the night went well for Bruce and Mom.

Thursday, November 18, 2004

Mom had bath-time scheduled, and she said no at first, but then our bath lady talked her into it. Mom said she was smart, and she felt a lot better. Mom slept a lot today. I didn't have to stay at Mom's last night. It was great being at home with my family and my own surroundings. It is hard not to think about mom. I need this time for me.

I'm back at Mom's for my shift. We talked about what we think heaven is like. I told her, "There is no pain, no pills, and no cancer in heaven, Mom—just happiness."

Her eyes lit up and she replied, "That's right. I had forgotten about that." Taking care of a dying loved one makes you so powerless. We just need the faith that we are all doing a good job. Keeping Mom in her own home has been a blessing, and we are lucky we can do this with twenty-four-hour care.

I think of the days when she sat in her fur coat or cooked a meal for someone who was hungry. I pray Mom's pain will be over soon, and then she will be with her loved ones who are waiting for her. She is walking some now. She takes slow and shuffled steps. She got ahold of the air freshener and pushed me out of the bathroom, closed the door, and kept spraying and spraying the air freshener. She was calling for the bath lady to come and help her. I was so scared for Mom. There will be

17

Brenda Ann Rebelein

no more air freshener and hair spray in the bathroom. Mom rested in the afternoon, and I read her some angel stories. Darcy had the night shift, and Mom wanted to walk. Darcy told her she could not walk around. They were by the bed, and it was lucky that Mom was facing the bed as she was standing and fell face down. Since mom didn't get hurt, they ended up giggling about it. They talked about how serious it could have been.

Friday, November 19, 2004

To us caretakers, company means a lot. When Mom visits with her company, she wants it to be light and fun, and mom seems to calm down when someone else is here. Today, Mom is very upset because we have taken her walker away. I moved it out of her bedroom. It's something like *out of sight out of mind*. Mom can't walk very well. This is so hard as we have never seen our Mom in this state of mind before. We will stay strong as a family and do what we have to for her. Today is another day. Mom's medication is not working. It is like the more we give her, the wilder she gets. Mom has one of those old-fashioned, heavy commodes. She was so mad at me for not giving her the walker that she started using the heavy commode for a walker. She walked the house from 9:30-2:30. I could not calm her down. At times, she was so angry with me. I can not blame Mom. This is the cancer controlling our lives. I called the hospice office, and the nurses were on their house visits. There was this angel on the other end of the phone telling me I was doing a good job, and she promised we would do something different with Mom's medication.

After Mom's five-hour walk, she went to sleep for a few hours. I went out for supper and did a little shopping. My cell phone rang, and it was Bruce. Mom was taking off her clothes and wanting to take a shower. I told Bruce to put Mom on the phone. "Mom, what are you doing? You had a bath today. Can you wait? I'm on my way, and I will help you." She told me she would wait. She would get her hair done while she was waiting for me to get there. We went right to Mom's. The hall light was on, Mom was sitting on the bed, and Bruce was putting curlers in her hair. By the look Bruce gave me, I think he was glad to see me. I had Mike and Bruce go outside for some fresh air. Mike helped us with Mom for awhile. Mike and I talked, and he thought I should

Living for the Moment

spend the night with Bruce in case it became a long night. Then Mike went home.

Mom has been talking about people from her childhood and past. I could cry for the pain she would be in if she knew how she was acting. She's talking so weirdly. We don't know what she is trying to say. We've had to put Mom in bed numerous times, and she just gets back up. We ended up calling Sheila. The truth is, we told her we needed a word search book because it was going to be a long night, but once we got her into the house, we locked the door and told she was not going anywhere. Mom fell on the floor, but she did not get hurt. Bruce called hospice at 11:00. They told us we should give her the emergency medication. Finally, at 2:00 a.m., Mom laid down, went to sleep, and stayed in bed. It was strange how whenever Sheila was sitting next to Mom, she would stay calm. We are so lucky we have each other.

Saturday, November 20, 2004

I stayed with Mom since she is a handful right now. Our hospice nurse came and redid Mom's medication. She informed us that we could put Mom in the hospital to get her settled down and to give the caretakers a break. Our nurse gave us a new drug for restlessness. We call it our miracle drug because it has worked. Each patient is different, and the drug we gave Mom before did not work, but for the next person it may help. You can't know unless you try it. We pray we never see that drug again. We decided to keep Mom at home because we hated to think of her in the hospital all alone. There is nothing they can do for her. She is resting well now. I went home, and Chuck stayed the night. She was quiet the rest of the night. Chuck said it was because he was there. We'll save that discussion for another day.

Sunday, November 21, 2004

Mom thought she smelled smoke in the middle of the night, but the new medication is working, and for the most part, Mom is talking and understanding and acting very calm. She ate well today. She read the newspaper. Even her mind is good today. She called a few people and held good conversations with them. She struggles with phone numbers, though. She tries to do it herself first, and then, if she can't do it, she will ask for help. Sundays are "Mom and me" days to spend together. I

19

Brenda Ann Rebelein

always stay a double shift on Sundays. I love my Mom so much, and I treasure each day we have together. She has really calmed down. We've got our mom back again. We love this new medication, which we got thanks to hospice.

Mom is weak and tired. It is understandable, though, considering what she has been through the last few days. She had me send a joke gift to her friends in Arizona. Mom still wants the last laugh.

Today was a dream come true. Mom had a good nap, and when she got up, we had a nice visit before she called to have some friends come over to see her. We have all missed the mom and grandma we know.

I noticed Mom has a few purple spots on her legs.

She was in a funny mood tonight. Chuck and Mom were teasing each other. We had lots of laughs tonight. What better medicine. Today was a perfect day.

Monday, November 22, 2004

Mom slept all night long. I still sleep in the recliner next to Mom's bed, just in case she gets up in the middle of the night. Our Mom is back. We see her humor and kindness. It is like getting a second chance. Mom got her bath and her hair done, and the nurse was here.

This is all so scary. When we leave her after a shift, we never know what it will be like when we get back. We just have to live for the moment and be strong. Mom told me, "You look like a nervous wreck. You need to go and talk to someone. I don't know if I can help you right now. You need to get stronger if you are going to make it through this ordeal." I promised Mom I would get strong.

Tuesday, November 23, 2004

Today was a treat day for me. I was home alone at my house for the day. I will not feel guilty because I'm not at Mom's. I go there tonight anyway. Jeanette and Mom are baking cookies today—or, I should say, Jeanette is baking, and Mom is giving orders because she is getting back to being the old mom. She loves the smell of fresh baked goodies coming out of the oven, and they are getting ready for Thanksgiving Day.

Mom is sleeping a lot more now. I pray each day that she will fall asleep and find the Lord. Today is the day Mom had picked to pass away. It is hard not to think about it when we just got over a bad reaction to that medication. It was hard because I was the only one who knew what date she had picked. I do not think she will die today. Mom made the comment yesterday that there are times she is scared, but she puts on a front like she is so happy all the time. I can not imagine what she is going through. We will be there to hold her hand.

When I got to Mom's house, Jeanette and Mom were having a good time. They were laughing and sharing secrets like they always have. It is times like this that I think we have more time with Mom than we thought. Mom was very alert tonight. She was talking about local people and the fun times they had. After that, she read her basket of cards which she receives each day.

Mom's laugh has changed. It used to be more of a hearty laugh.

I went into Mom's bedroom and asked her if she knew what the date was. She did because she told me today it was the day she was supposed to die. Mom, being the card that she is, stuck out her tongue and acted like she was dead.

She is still weak, but she is walking more with the help of a walker.

Mom woke up in the middle of the night screaming for Darcy. Mom said she had seen a black dog running through the house, and she was so sure he was still in the house. We had to go from room to room and check all of the locked doors. Finally, Mom calmed down and was ready to go back to bed. I told her it was 12:07 a.m. She did not die on the day she had guessed. Mom and I had a good laugh as she thinks that momma knows best. She slept but was restless all night.

Wednesday, November 24, 2004

Mom woke up sick to her stomach and weak.

It is hard to leave her each day. I just need to learn to grab my overnight bag and go. I went and had lunch with my girlfriends. It was fun having some girl time.

I'm having an IBS attack, so I'm going home to bed. I need the rest of the day to take care of me. Mom is eating cornflakes with Darcy.

Thanksgiving is tomorrow. We will get together for our last Thanksgiving with Mom. This is a gift from God. We didn't think she would make it until Thanksgiving Day.

21

Brenda Ann Rebelein

Thursday, November 25, 2004

Today is Thanksgiving Day. We have a lot to be grateful for. Darcy and Chuck made oyster stew as this is our family tradition. Jade, Darcy and Jeremy's oldest daughter, made her first two pumpkin pies, and they turned out good.

Today it was hard seeing Mom just lying in bed. She has always been the life of our parties. She has this uplifted personality. She also hollers when it is time to eat, and we all come running because she is not going to say it twice. Mom always did all the cooking for our get-togethers. She would not want it any other way. Mom tried to get up a couple of times, but she realized she could not do it, so back in bed she would go. We all took turns going in her bedroom to visit with her.

Just having her look up at me, smiling, was all I needed. Mom said she was enjoying lying there and listening to her family. She knows now we will all be okay when she is gone. My IBS is acting up from thinking about how I need to face what holidays will be like without mom. I just need to learn to enjoy this moment. We had good food, and being together as a family was a lot to be thankful for.

Friday, November 26, 2004

I did not go to Mom's today. I went shopping and out for lunch. Mary Lou is with her today. Mom had a good day.

Tonight she was doing a lot of vomiting. Bruce was with, and he called hospice, and they changed her medication. Mike and I have a snow removal business, and they are calling for snow for the night. I will take what is given to me. God may want me to take a day to work hard for a change.

One day at a time.

Saturday, November 27, 2004

Well, we got a nice big snowstorm. I worked with Mike. Darcy and the girls were with Mom. They had a great day. Mom was in a good mood, and the medication was working. Darcy's girls are younger, so when it's her night to stay, they come with her and go to school from their grandma's house. They feel helpful when they are taking care of their grandma. They rub her feet and polish her nails, all things she

22

Living for the Moment

needs done. Mom was eating warm milk toast when I got there. Mom has always loved warm milk toast.

She was very testy with me because she had wanted me there hours ago. I did feel bad that I had missed her good hours. I'm glad Darcy and the girls had a wonderful day with Mom. We will have good and bad days. The good ones are a blessing from God. Mike and Josh have been so understanding through this situation. Monica and Desiree and Destiny always cheer me up. Lance and Kristine always let me vent to them. I'm so lucky I have the family that I have. I love each one of them.

Sunday, November 28, 2004

Mom and I had a great day today. She was herself today. We had a good talk about the future and what it will be like without her. She told me she wants my daughter, Monica, to buy the house.

Vicki, Sheila, Miranda, Monica and Aurora are good about bringing the little ones to see mom. Chuck and Thelma's daughter, Vicki and her husband Pete, and kids Pat, Alecia, Ashley, Jon, Amanda and Alexis came to spend the day with mom.

Mom was in a teasing mood today later in the day. We had fun, and on Sundays we always have a lot of company. She got all dressed up and fixed her hair all pretty. She likes to look nice when people stop in. Chuck and Thelma served Mom and me pork chops with all the trimmings. Mom fixed her plate up and ate what she could. When they were leaving, Mom wanted to flash them from her big picture window, but she was in her wheelchair, and I could not get to the window fast enough. Mom thought I was hopeless as she laughed her hearty laugh.

Today was a very unforgettable day for me. Mom gave me so much to think about. Everyone that visits or stays with Mom gets these moments that last a lifetime.

Monday, November 29, 2004

Mom slept all night. One time, her breathing got rather funny, but then it went back to normal again. She didn't called for me all night. Caretakers sleep in the bedroom next to Mom's bedroom, though I have still been sleeping in the chair next to her bed. Mike says I can

Brenda Ann Rebelein

sleep anywhere. She likes it when I sleep in the chair, and sometimes, in the middle of the night, we will talk. She likes her favorite radio station on while she sleeps or takes naps. The first night we had the music on all night, Mom was sleeping in her bed and I was in my chair. It was dark, with only a night-light on, when the song, "I'm So Lonesome I Could Cry," came on. I had to laugh. Talk about depressing music. Mom listens to this every night just hoping her and Dad's song comes on from when they first started dating, "Sentimental Journey." She can be sleeping, and that song will wake her right up.

I guess Mom thought she heard me snoring. This morning when we woke up, she told me to get her purse. She doesn't mind if I sleep in the chair, but I will have to go buy some snore strips. I asked her if she heard me snoring and why she didn't just wake me up. She thinks I work too hard and that I needed my sleep.

Mom had so much company today, and she loves it. She makes sure everyone gets enough coffee and something good to eat. She had grandchildren, friends and family here. Jeanette arrived with all of her baking supplies, something Mom and Jeanette both look forward to. Today's special is Mom's favorite sugar cookies. Jeanette and Mom had a good day. Darcy and the girls were there for the night, and they had good time. We are so lucky. We are all getting this time to build more memories.

Tuesday, November 30, 2004

I got called to Mom's to take care of her. Jeanette had an emergency, so I'm here for a double shift. Mom is doing well. She had a bath, Candy fixed her hair, and the makeup looks good. The nurse was here. We can call if we have any questions, and she will come back in a month unless we need her. Mom is as sharp as a tack today. I will be here until tomorrow night. I do miss my family, but this is just something I need to do right now.

Each member of my family always makes me feel better. Chuck and Thelma came for supper. Chuck and I made a pasta supper with chicken and seafood. It was awesome. I never thought I would see the day that Chuck and I would be in the kitchen cooking together. We could hear Mom laughing. Mom has always been our cook. She thinks we can not cook, but we showed her tonight. It was a great time. Mom did not have time for a nap as we kept her too busy.

Hospice has a routine that has helped us so much. On certain day's, Mom gets a bath, and they change the bedding. The nurse is always checking on us and reading our daily medical journal to see how the medications are working. The social workers are making sure we are all okay and seeing if anyone needs to talk. Hospice is there for us twenty-four hours a day.

I wrote this letter to Mom and will read it to her when I know the time is right. I wrote this on a day when she was so tired and weak.

LETTER TO MY MOM

Dear Mom,

This is so hard to begin as I watch you sleep near me. I know God will give me the words that I need to express my love. Mom, you have given me everything—your love and your strength. The main thing you taught me is to be a woman and a mom just like you. We have had so many good times and some bad. I need to say that I'm sorry for the bad and whenever I have been wrong. You never turned your back on me. You never looked down on me when I was learning my lessons in life. You always stood by me to teach me right from wrong, no matter how old I was. It was a great warm feeling, knowing you were by my side. God bless you for your motherhood.

The good times are too numerous to mention them all, but here are a few: growing up, working side by side in the restaurant business, trips to Las Vegas, Christmas time together as a big family, the awesome food, talking on the phone, or birthday-time at Morton. It will not be the same. I will have your coat and purse with me, as you requested, so I can win the big pot at the casino. I do hope the monkeys will be good to me since they are our favorite slot. We will all be okay, so don't worry a bit. We are glad your pain will be over soon, as God will be calling for you. I will not

Brenda Ann Rebelein

say goodbye because that is too final. I will say I love you, and we will meet again. God bless you and your journey. I pray that I will be just like you, and you have given me the tools.

Love,
Your daughter, Brenda

Chapter 3

Wishes Do Come True

December 2004

We are facing the fourth month of our cancer journey. We are pulling together to make this happen, being with Mom in her own home. We have so many friends and family circling around us. Mom wants a few things to happen. We call it her wish list, and this is the month for wishes since it is December. It's in God's hands.

Wednesday, December 1, 2004

I stayed overnight with Mom last night. We both slept all night. It's funny. Every night that I stay at Mom's, she checks my nose and points her index finger to see if I have a nose strip on for my snoring. When Mom means business, she shakes her index finger. It also means Mom (or Grandma) has spoken.

Mom had a big day yesterday, so she is tired today. Yesterday was a good day. She woke up alert this morning, not confused like some mornings. She had her bath given to her by her favorite bath lady from hospice. We had lunch and watched Mom's favorite soap operas. I had to remind her about what was going on, and some of it I just guessed at. Mom wanted some alone time in her bedroom. She told me to leave the light on.

Mom is still in her teasing mood. She has this new hearty laugh that warms my heart. You would have to know mom to understand her. Her door is always open a crack when she rests. She has a large night stand full of stuff next to her bed, and she will go through those baskets and boxes for hours. Mom loves to polish her nails also.

Mom talked to me again about one of her wishes. It was for Monica to buy her house when she is gone. She also has plans for someone else, but she will not tell me who or what it is. She doesn't know if she will complete the wish before she passes away. If she doesn't get it done, she doesn't want this person to be disappointed, so if they never hear

27

Brenda Ann Rebelein

about it, they will never know. Mom has always had a caring heart, and she will live in us forever.

These last five days have been great. She was her old self. It is like she does not even have cancer. Mom got all of her jewelry out and put it on her dresser, and she wanted us to pick out what we wanted. She stood in the back and did not help us. She just watched to see what we liked. Every time someone came, she told them to go and get something, a pair of earrings or a necklace or maybe her favorite pin.

Last night, Mom told us the joke was on us kids. She is living high on the hog, and we are the dummies taking such good care of her. She's decided she just might go on for three more years living like this. We all just looked at her. It is good to see her enjoying the family and friends circled around her as we go on this journey together. Every day, Mom's kids and grandkids will call or stop in.

Mom had some quick catnaps today in her chair. She doesn't want to miss anything. Now she is putting duct tape on her wheelchair. Duct tape is the answer to everything in my Mom's eyes. I told her she will not survive heaven if there is no duct tape.

We had a great day. She had a lot of company again. People are so surprised at how well she is doing. The talk after Mom's one bad spell was that she didn't have much time left, but when they stop in, she is the life of the party. She still does her hair and makeup every day.

Bruce and Wendy's daughter, Aurora, stopped in with her little Mayson. He is one year old. Mom was happy to see them. He sat on Grandma's lap a long time, making a mess eating sugar cookies and drinking a little Coke. Mom kept telling him, "Brenda loves to clean messes up. Give us another sugar cookie." Soon he was standing next to Mom, and Aurora told Mayson, "Hurry up, honey, and eat your cookie and drink your pop. We have to go home." Mayson turned and looked at Aurora, and then he tipped his glass upside down on Mom's lap. After that, he headed for Aurora and grabbed his diaper bag and headed for the door. He did as he was told. It took us all by surprise. Mom laughed so hard. It made her day.

Tonight at suppertime, the church carolers came and sang to Mom. They filled the house up with adults and children of all ages. I taped it, and mom sang along as much as she could. They sang one of Mom's favorite songs, "Silent Night." Mom was so happy to see them. She told them she was going to beat this cancer and that she would be okay. Of course they could not leave without some homemade cookies. This gave Mom a lift. It warms our hearts that they went from house to house to those in need. I brought mom my angel, that folds her hands and sings "Silent Night."

Darcy and the girls stayed the night. Darcy and Mom had a good talk about Mom's upcoming death. It was good for both of them to talk this out. Our time with Mom alone is so special. When she has company, I like to give them their alone time. It's something they do not have to share with anyone. We all need to take this time and enjoy what we have left and make the best of it.

Thursday, December 2, 2004

I came to take care of Mom only until twelve o'clock, and then Jeanette will be coming in. She wanted to dress up in regular clothes because she's usually wearing sleepwear sets.

I do get scared when I leave. I think about what it will be like when I get back for another shift. We went through those bad weeks when we thought we were coming to the end. Will things spin out of control again? I need my faith because God has his plans for us. Mom has been so good to so many people. I feel He will not make her suffer. I called Mom's two closest friends, and they came over for coffee and treats. Their friendships have been strong for so many years, and I want them to spend as much time with Mom as they can. Each day is a gift, and we do not know what tomorrow brings. They had a good time.

Jeanette came with a small tree for the deck, and Mary Lou, put real wreaths on the rod railing on the deck. Mom said, "No big tree up this year," and that is all the decorating for Christmas she wanted. Her deck looks over the lake, and right now it looks so nice.

Jeanette is baking up a storm since it's Christmas. She is keeping us in baked goodies. It is time for Jeanette and Mom to have their time. They love to disagree—Mom being the cook and Jeanette the baker. They were having a good time when I left. I need this time with my family at home. I can see the difference in my home. The tension is running high here without me. I just need to stay focused, as Darcy says.

Brenda Ann Rebelein

Mom is talking and acting like she did six months ago, before she had this terrible disease. I just don't understand this disease.

It is a quiet night at home.

Friday, December 3, 2004

Mom wants to talk to the hospice nurse about her pain level. She asks for a pain pill but will not talk about the level of pain. Mom never complains. She has yet to say a negative thing about the life we are living. She called me three times last night, and I think she just wanted to talk. The phone has been a big thing for us in our relationship.

Mom got a call from a close friend. They go back many years, and their memories will be with them forever. She is doing well today. Hospice staff keeps reminding us to live for today. It is hard for me not to think of the future. This is when I need to slow myself down.

Mom's whole day went well. She had some close friends over for lunch. At suppertime, she was tired and somewhat confused. She misses her electric blanket. You can't have an electric blanket and oxygen together. She took the news better then I thought she would, and I know how she loves her electric blanket.

Mom did go through a lot of pain medication today. We will keep watching for any changes. Hospice reassured us that they would stay with us until the end. We are so lucky to have such wonderful people in our lives. Mom is doing well now. I know hospice only comes in if the patient does not have much time, and I was just worried if they would go away if Mom makes a turn for the better. But they promised me they would not leave us until the end of our journey.

Saturday, December 4, 2004

Mom only got up once to go to the bathroom. I had fallen asleep as I only have to be here for a few hours. Mom felt so bad for waking me up. She is always apologizing when she does things like that.

We all love her so much. Her heart is as big as a melon. My girlfriend called to talk to me because she has a surgery coming up, and it's a hard time for her. I was next to Mom, and she grabbed the phone from me and introduced herself. Mom knew the situation and told her calmly just how it was. It was just like Mom, short and sweet and to the point. They talked for awhile about the pros and the cons of the surgery. I

30

tried not to get tears in my eyes. She helped my girlfriend feel so much better and helped her get the strength she needed.

In the restaurant business, Mom was famous for her BBQ Ribs and her homemade sauce. She has a wish to teach Chuck how to make them before she gets too sick. Today, they did some planning on making the sauce and what they needed. Mom is focusing very hard on getting this task completed. We know the timing has to be just right. Once she has her mind set on something, she will not stop until it is completed.

Mom was starting to get a little restless right before I left. Chuck gave her a pill for her restlessness, and it settled her down. They were having a good time in the kitchen after that little spell. Mom was sitting on her little stool, and Chuck was doing the work. I bet he had to do it just right as we've all had to when we worked for her.

Mike and I celebrated our wedding anniversary tonight even though it is tomorrow. Mom and Chuck called. They are serving us Mom's BBQ Ribs made by Charles, a wish that does come true.

Sunday, December 5, 2004

Mike surprised me with diamond earrings. We went out for supper with Jim and Jeanette. I had to call Mom right away last night. If anything happens in my life, my Mom is the first one I call. She knew all about it, and she told me that I deserve them and to enjoy them.

Chuck made BBQ Ribs for the family. Mom was glowing in the kitchen. Her Ribs were priceless. She was giggling at Chuck as she had him so busy in the kitchen being a great host. Yes, Mom also taught Chuck that when you make an outstanding meal, you also make a big mess. I had dish duty. We had a good time considering we don't know how much time we have left with our mom and grandma. When everyone was gone, Mom and I had a good time alone.

At 1:00 a.m., Mom screamed, "Fire!" I was in a deep sleep when she woke me up. I had to prove to her that there was no fire and that we were safe, but I finally calmed her down. She had read in the paper yesterday about a fire that happened to her friend's house 35 years ago. We will take each day as it is dealt to us.

Monday, December 6, 2004

Mom ended up getting out of bed three times. She is having her bath and getting her bed changed, and the nurse will visit. Candy is coming to do her hair. Every other Monday, Mom has her hair done. She's even doing some cooking, but we stand next to her to make sure she does not get hurt. Cooking has always been Mom's enjoyment.

I'm at home now, and sometimes when I come home, it is like I'm seeing things for the first time. I love my home. It is a special place to be. The guys are doing an awesome job with the housework duties. I always come home to a clean house. I just need to get caught up on the laundry. Before this is over, I may introduce them to the washer and dryer. Is it bad for me to think that I will be glad when this is over? Mom is doing so well now. We are just getting so tired. There is so much to do. We have jobs to go to, schedules to arrange with Mom, and our own houses to keep going. I will rest, and then I will feel better. The hospice nurse was at Mom's and changed her medication because of the hallucinations.

Tuesday, December 7, 2004

I have the day shift at Mom's today. She's in a lot of pain in her head and neck. We got her a spa neck wrap that we're keeping warm around her neck. This has helped, and I see they increased her pain medication.

Mom did have a good afternoon. She loves sitting in her dining room in her chair and looking out at the lake. She had a few bites of food. Mom said she is going to send us a sign from heaven once she gets there. She told all of us that she is coming back as a yellow butterfly. "How will we know it is you?" I asked.

She pointed her index finger at me. "Oh, you will know. Believe me. I will stand out from all the other ones." Mom said the first meal she would make in heaven was her liver and onions that everyone loves. "I know your dad will kiss and love me all up for that," she said. Then we talked about what we both thought heaven was like. Everyone has his or her own thoughts on that one. Mom is so open about dying. She seems to be facing this head-on. She has had a good life, and she is so ready to move on and see what's on the other side. I was surprised when she told me that the person she will be the happiest to see is her grandma. She laughs about the fun she will have in heaven, but when the time comes, she will have to go in peace and let the control go to a higher power.

I told Mom that I have a friend in Boston who is expecting a baby. "That's nice. For every death there is a birth. I would love to make room in this world for your friend's little one," she told me. Mom is so unselfish. She never fails to amaze me with her kindness.

Wednesday, December 8, 2004

Today was a big day for us. Chuck is having a surprise birthday party for his wife, Thelma. Mom had talked all this time about how she would be at that party. Medically, I could not see that happening since sometimes she gets restless at the drop of a hat. We are really are just living for the moment. I have so many mixed feelings about this. I need to write my thoughts now.

There will be so many people there. She is hard to handle even though at the moment she is doing well. She can't handle much noise at times anymore, even with little kids. Mom is in a wheelchair and her feet flare up. I don't want to take this day away from her, but she has been restless and uncomfortable today. She had her medication in the afternoon as scheduled. This party starts at 6:00. Mom gets ready for bed at 7:00. I'm here by myself.

Today it is cold out, and the wind is blowing. These are my feelings. Are they wrong? Family and friends are calling to see if Mom is coming to the party. They will come and help if needed. I told them that Mom was sleeping and that she was comfortable. I did not think we would make it. The calls were coming still coming in at 5:45. Mom had been sleeping all afternoon and had not moved except for her medication.

I was at the dining room table. I could see into Mom's bedroom. She had been sleeping the last four hours. Suddenly she screamed to me, "Help me! It's time to go to a party!" As I turned my head, the covers were flying into the air. Mom jumped up and sat on the side of the bed. "What should I wear so I'll look nice? Oh, and grab my fur coat."

I'm sure I stood there dumbfounded. No words would come out. I got her black sweater with the scarf that Darcy gave her and her cancer pin and her white pants and, of course, her fur coat. She did her hair

33

Brenda Ann Rebelein

and makeup. Mom had this unknown strength. I can not tell you the emotions I had. I didn't have time to call anyone because I was busy getting this fancy lady ready for a party. Mom didn't want to make a big deal out of her coming to the party since the party was for Thelma. I told Mom I was nervous going alone with her. She said, "It will be okay, and I promise I will behave. Just give me one hour there. When I look at you and say, 'Brenda,' you'll know that I'm ready to go. That will be our sign. Do you think one hour is okay? Let's not make a scene as this is Thelma's day. I just want to be with people for a few minutes."

I looked at Mom with this amazed look. We have all wondered where she gets all this unknown energy. It's not that we want her to be down. It is just one extreme to the next, and we don't understand any of this. We are just living day by day and taking what is given to us.

So off to the car we went. Yes, I prayed all the way to the car with Mom, being careful at every step. On the way, Mom asked me if she looked like a dying woman. I told her she looked beautiful. "Wait until everyone sees you!" I said. I had time to call Mike and say that we'd be there in ten minutes. "Be by the door and help me with Mom," I told him.

They could not believe Mom was there, and all the family and friends were already there. Mike and Jeremy, Darcy's husband, greeted us. We walked into the party, and there were cheers and clapping of hands as Mom came through the door in the wheelchair with her fur coat on, looking like a million dollars! The look on some people's faces was priceless. We never dreamed Mom would make it to this party.

This was another wish Mom had hoped for, to attend one last party. Word was out that Mom had a bad reaction to that medication and that she did not have much time left. But she surprised us once again. Mom got so many hugs and kisses. She was having a good time. It was weird, though, how when I was at the table next to Mom, we looked at each other, and we both knew it was time to go without saying any words.

I was glad we went. Sometimes we need to step out of our comfort zone. When we got back to town, she wanted to drive around and look at everyone's Christmas lights on their houses. We were gone for an hour and a half, and when we got home, Mom was very tired but satisfied. We went to bed right away. I know we thought we were lucky that Mom made it until Thanksgiving, but now she has faced Thelma's

Living for the Moment

birthday, and we are just a couple of weeks from Christmas. Tonight was a gift and a memorable evening for everyone.

Thursday, December 9, 2004

We got up once last night for the bathroom. We both slept in this morning. Mom is tired today; yesterday was a big day for her.

The medication is going well. Mom is not as confused as she was. Later in the afternoon, she had a table full of close friends. They were talking about the good old days.

I had to get caught up on the laundry, so I told Mom to behave while I was in the basement for a few minutes. When I got upstairs, Mom was in the bathroom running water full force and putting a wash cloth in her mouth. I looked at her, puzzled. I did not know what she was doing. She kept throwing water with a cloth in her mouth. She pointed to a tube of dental grip for false teeth. Mom has lost about 50 lbs. so far. Her teeth are getting loose since she has lost so much weight. She had used too much dental grip, and her mouth was being gripped shut. We were laughing so hard as we tried to keep her mouth open. This would have been good on camera. Finally, it broke loose. It was like paste. I bet she never does that again. We laughed all day, every time she had to spit more of that junk out of her mouth.

Mom and Darcy are planning a clothes-shopping trip. They both love buying new clothes. Mom looked so beautiful last night. People have commented during this journey that Mom's looks have not changed. Everyone knows that appearance is a big thing for Mom. That is why when she gets close to meeting her maker, she only wants us kids to see her. She wants people to think about how she lived and not how she dies.

Mom has faced this cancer head on. She came home from the hospital to have those final happy moments for us to remember her by. Mom had a quiet night. She was tired from last night. I was glad she could make the party. God helped us through the night.

Friday, December 10, to Tuesday, December 14, 2004

I came down with a bad flu. I think it is God saying it's time for me to take better care of myself. I will not be staying at Mom's until I'm better. I miss her dearly, but it is time for other people to have their time with her. She's calling me three to five times a day. It's good to hear her voice. At times she sounds so weak, but then the next time she calls, she sounds normal. Each of us has our own connection with Mom, and Grandma, that we will always cherish. I have gone from being there every day to not being there, and that is hard for me to accept. We both feel empty not being together. We have become so close through this journey. I know I have been accused of being over-protective. It's me. I want to save her, and I need to accept that this is out of my control. I only have one Mom, and I want to be with her as long as I can. It is like we have changed roles. She was always there for me, and now it is my turn to be there for her. I know she trusts me, and sometimes I do let her do things that I probably shouldn't. We like to stay up late at night, but what could that hurt?

I feel bad at times when I think this will all be over soon. Right now I can go over to Mom's and she is there. The nurse was there this week, and nothing has changed in a month. Mom's mediation is working well, so that will stay the same. Chuck, Bruce, Darcy, Mary Lou and Jeanette had to take my shifts. They said Mom is getting a little more forgetful. She is sleeping a lot more during the day. Mom is makes quick jumps when she is lying down resting.

Mom still has a great attitude. Here I should be cheering her up, and she is helping me. She can tell that I feel down because I can't be there right now to help her. Mom always seems to know the right thing to say. I pray some day I can be like my mom, but there is only one Marvel Mae.

Darcy called me at 8:30 tonight. "You'll never guess what we're doing!" she said. "We're frying liver and onions. Mom was hungry for it." I wished her luck. She called me after she had Mom in bed. She said it was the best meal Mom had ever made. They had a few people stop in, so they joined them in another delicious meal made by Mom. Chuck and Mom also worked on making some more BBQ Ribs for Christmas. I bet Mom was sitting on her stool being the boss. I love taking one day at a time.

Living for the Moment

Wednesday, December 15, 2004

I'm finally back doing shifts at Mom's. It is good being back at home. This is the house we all grew up in. It seems like I have been gone forever.

The bath lady was here. Mom has a very bad hangnail on her big toe. You can see that it's infected and sore. I hope to remove it myself because I have a trick. I use anbesol to just numb the toe and then pull it out. I was sitting on the floor with her foot on my lap and my nose up to her toe when Mom let out a big scream and jumped. I screamed with her. Boy, did she get a good laugh scaring me. Mom is amazed that her toe doesn't hurt any more.

Mike stopped in at Mom's. He has done all our Christmas shopping. He told me my hands are full taking care of Mom, so it is something I do not have to think about. The gifts are all bought. What would I do without him during this time? Mom is trying to teach me how to cook BBQ Ribs. I can not believe how she is still teaching us about cooking or teaching us about life. She is always turning everything into something positive.

They had another medication change while I was gone. The hospice nurse is giving Mom anxiety medication to help Mom at bedtime since her bad fire dreams. I will enjoy this day with her. She wants to get some cards and letters out to people she has been thinking of. She wants to give them an update on her condition. Mom was rather restless tonight. She ordered two more cases of Ribs tonight. She is used to cooking in the restaurant business where everything is in cases. She has plans to get them done so people who have been good to her will get ribs for Christmas made by her. She is so proud of her BBQ Ribs. She has passed the recipe down to only Chuck, and then he can pick someone to pass it down to. This has always been a dream for Mom. Dreams do come true.

Thursday, December 16, 2004

Christmas is coming soon. I think Mom will make it until Christmas. We are getting a miracle to have Mom this long. When they said it was a fast acting cancer and she did not have much time left, I thought she would be gone right away. We have had time to prepare ourselves for this. We will be blessed with one more Christmas as a family.

Brenda Ann Rebelein

Mom woke me up this morning. She is very antsy. We were up at 3:30 a.m. to use the bathroom and then three more times by 7:00.

Mom was resting. Jeanette and I were having some morning coffee together. I think that was bothering Mom. It was always Jeanette and Mom, and now we are having coffee together since Mom is in bed. I could tell this upset Mom, so I left for work.

Jeanette stopped at my house on the way home when her shift was done at Mom's. It was a bad day at Mom's today. Mom was very weak and insisted on walking to the kitchen to make more ribs. When Mom has her mind set on something, nothing can change it. It is at times like this when she knows she is losing control of herself, the cancer, and the medication. It was a bad day for them. It is hard having these days when Mom has to fight anxiety. Mom is sick and fighting for her life. It has to be a terrible feeling. We have all worked these shifts. She is hard to handle on these days. It can change so quickly from one minute to the next. Mom only had a twenty-minute nap then she was on the go. Darcy is with her tonight, and I will go there in the morning. God will only give us what we can handle. We are so lucky to be a team to help each other through the good and bad days.

Friday, December 17, 2004

Mom had a good night last night. That was good to hear. I relieved Darcy and the girls. Mom went back to bed this morning after being up for a few minutes. She has been doing this a lot lately. It is too much for her to get up and start her day right away.

I do not hold back on medication any more. If Mom needs it, I will not second-guess myself. I know I'm doing the right thing. I want her to be comfortable so we can handle the situation. Bruce has been kept busy taking care of Mom's bedroom phone. I bet he wishes he could have a quarter for every time we have had him connect and disconnect Mom's phone in the bedroom. With Mom being so antsy, we have tried to keep the ringer off, so she will rest. She will be in a sound sleep when the phone rings and in one shot, she is up and grabbing the phone. Weakness has nothing to do with it at this point. The phone agitates her for some reason. When it works and when it does not. The minute she can not get a dial tone, she is calling Bruce from another phone to fix her phone.

Living for the Moment

Mom is tired today. She does remember her bad day yesterday. She is having a hard time staying awake. Bruce stops every day to see how things are going and if we need anything. Some times we are low on medications. We are always needing a medication run. Thelma, Sheila and Mike are picking up a lot of the medication, too.

Mom and Bruce both like to play solitaire. They argue about who is cheating and who is not. I told them that I think they both are probably cheating.

Chuck relieved me tonight. They were going to have ribs for supper. Mom only eats a few bites of food. They went to bed early.

Saturday, December 18, 2004

I relieved Chuck this morning. Mom slept all night long. Mom is sleeping a lot in her chair in the dining room. The hospice nurse told her she should take little catnaps any place she is sitting just so she is comfortable. Mom was happy that she got the okay. She looks so tired and run down today. I do not know if Mom is reaching another stage in her cancer journey. She did eat some egg salad on a rosette. She learned that from her mother who loved eating that around Christmas time also.

Mom was sitting at the dining room table playing solitaire. She was confused and holding a conversation, and I was watching her play cards. She knew the next move. She played until her fingers would not work any more, then she was off for a nap. Mom is talking a lot, but then she loses her train of thought. She went to bed early. She could not stay awake.

Sunday, December 19, 2004

Mom slept all night long last night. She told me she thinks she will stay in bed all day, as she is so tired and weak. She asked me if it was Sunday today. I told her it was. She wants some nice clothes out in case she gets extra company. Sunday is a good visiting day. Mom looks forward to her company.

She prays she will die on a Sunday. That would be a good day to go home, she is always telling us. I'm so amazed at Mom with her attitude. She never says a negative word. She is always looking at what we will be facing next. *Dear God, give me some of the strength my mom has.*

39

Brenda Ann Rebelein

I can see mom is worse. She told me she feels herself slipping, and she gave me the talk about how I need to toughen up. I need to stay strong. Each day that we are given is so precious. At times we see her slipping, but then at other times she's jumping up with extra energy. This is all in God's hands. I need to accept things for what they are. Mom's voice is so weak that I have to really listen close to her at times. Mom has always had control, and soon she will have to give up the driving reins to someone else named our Lord Jesus.

Mom stayed the same all day. She stayed in bed all day today. She had some sharp pains. I convinced her to stay in bed and said that if she got company, it was okay for them to come to her and visit in her bedroom. They wouldn't mind since they're coming to see her.

Reading has always been one of her favorite past times. She loves going to bed early and snuggling up with a good romance book. She was trying to read so hard. If she gets a paragraph read, she is so happy before she falls asleep.

Monday, December 20, 2004

In the medical journal we have to keep for hospice, we note how Mom is doing and any changes in the medication. I usually put a positive note on top to start our day. Then when I stop doing it, I see that everyone misses it. They all tease me about it, but they read the wisdom for the day.

I need to slow things down for me; I'm getting so tired. Mom has been my strength all my life and now it is my time to be her strength and someone she can count on. I have prayed a long time that I would get the chance to repay her for all she did for me, and now is the time.

I will not be at Mom's today. I will have to work with Mike in our snow removal business.

Mom had a big day today. Her friends arrived from Arizona. They came home for Christmas to be with family. Mom needs them right now as I'm sure they need her. It is time for them to be together and have their final moments. Chuck made BBQ Ribs for supper for them. They stayed the night with Mom and Chuck.

Mom played a joke on Chuck tonight. She found some pills in a little box on her bed stand, poured them out, and was counting them over and over. Chuck wondered what she was doing and if she was losing it. Meanwhile, she was watching Chuck and giggling inside. She called to tell me what she had done. I called Chuck and told him to throw the old pills away. They were all having a good time in Mom's bedroom. It was good to hear her happy tonight.

Tuesday, December 21, 2004

We moved snow all day today. I called to see how things were going at Mom's. Mary Lou, is the caretaker today. Bruce and his son, Spenser, have the night shift. Mom was very tired today. She's been eating a lot of soup. Mom loves soup. Darcy has been good about bringing homemade soup to Mom, and I have been making us homemade hamburger soup.

Mom had her bath and got her hair done. She got to talk to Doctor Mohr today from Rochester. She was so happy. She had to call me and tell me. She told him she was still going strong. They have had a patient/friend relationship for twenty years. She is always talking about how much he has meant to her.

I stayed home and worked. The snow is a blessing for me right now.

Wednesday, December 22, 2004

Mom is eating very little now. It is hard to see this woman who was surrounded with cooking all her life barely able to swallow. Since we have been staying with her, we bring our own food in. It is easier for everyone, but mainly for Mom. When she knows someone comes to her house hungry, she wants to be in the kitchen, no matter how weak or sick she is. On the good days, it is okay, but on the bad days, it can get dangerous. We need to keep her out of harm's way.

Mom slept all day today. She is having more troubles with itching. We called hospice, and they took care of it right away. Hospice is so wonderful. It was pretty quiet today.

Thursday, December 23, 2004

Mom did not get up all day today. She is very tired and weak. It is hard for Mom to walk. Her feet are very swollen. She is staying in bed and only gets up to use the commode next to her bed.

Brenda Ann Rebelein

Friday, December 24, 2004

It's Christmas Eve. We have always had our kids home for Christmas. On Christmas Day, we all go to Mom's. It is a miracle that God has given us one more Christmas to be together. Mom said this Christmas will be like any other year. She wants her house filled up with adults and kids—the more the merrier. If she gets sick of us, she will just shut her bedroom door.

The only thing that she felt bad about was not being able to put out her usual feast. We told her we would bring everything; she should just enjoy herself. She can lie down when she gets tired. There will be no gifts. It is our day just to be together. We should all come casual. She just wants to see her family.

We had the kids come home to our house. We did our own traditions. It was a good Christmas here, and we watched our granddaughters opening their gifts one at a time, excitedly anticipating the next gift. There was paper every where. That's what Christmas is all about. Monica, our daughter, went to spend the night with Mom. They had another medication change. Mom is having some pain with arthritis in her wrists and feet. This is time for Monica and Grandma to be together. Each grandchild is having their own time with Grandma, and it is so important to them all. This is like a waiting game. I tell my kids to prepare themselves, make the best of it, treat it as the last time they will see her, and make it special. I tell them to remember the good times. You never know when things can change, and we have to just live for the moment.

Saturday, December 25, 2004

Merry Christmas to all. This cancer journey has made everyone stronger and better people. Family and friends have pulled together as one. We got our wish. Mom made it until Christmas Day. I thank God for making this happen. We are having a potluck. We are having oyster stew, our family tradition. For years, Mom did all the cooking and would not let us help her. It was something she always loved doing for her family. I always went and helped her set the tables, and there are forty-two of us in the family. She always inspected my work. I'm having flashbacks of us working in the restaurant together for so many years. Mom would put out a feast. She would serve three kinds of meats

42

Living for the Moment

(duck, goose and ham), mash potatoes, gravy, corn, and green beans. I was allowed to bring my baked beans, stuffing, salads, and relish trays. Then everyone could bring a dessert to pass. We had it family style, set up in the kitchen. She would only holler once when the food was ready, and Bruce would have to deliver food to people that lived alone before we could eat. What a zoo this house was when we all got together. How many people always asked us where we put everyone? It is home. Mom never focused on the food and the gifts, just bringing everyone home. One last Christmas together... We always play games. They always fight over me being on their team. Okay, so maybe they don't.

Earlier this morning, Mom's hospice nurse came with her husband and received her roaster full of Chuck and Mom's BBQ ribs. They were so proud of themselves for having completed their task of Chuck learning how to do Mom's Ribs.

Since we were all dressing casually, I wore a pink sweat outfit. When we arrived at Mom's, there were a lot of people there. This was the first time that I was not the first one there. When we came in the house, Darcy was kneeling next to Mom and having her picture taken. "Good. Brenda is here just in time to have her picture taken with us," I heard my sister say. I was the last person to come in the house. There was Mom in her chair with Darcy next to her, and they were both wearing pink sweat suits. We all laughed. Everyone thought we had planned this out. We were all surprised. We had our picture taken together. We were the ladies in pink. This is a picture Darcy and I will cherish forever. We were passing out copies. Courtney and Sheila made us some extras ones. Mom told me to put it in the local paper a year from now when she is gone and tell her how much we miss her.

Mom was up most of the day. When she would go rest, we would try to be quiet. We also checked on her frequently, and she told us, "I just enjoy laying here, listening to my family, knowing that you will all be fine once I'm gone. That makes me happy. Always stay together." Mom lay there and smiled and gave our hands a quick squeeze. The kids all went and talked with Grandma, and some just crawled right up in bed with her. It's a blessing that none of the kids were scared. It can be scary when a loved one is sick when you're little.

It was good that she was not in the hospital and we had the comfort of her home. I did leave in the late afternoon. It was hard for me to face

Brenda Ann Rebelein

that this was our last Christmas together. I was getting weak. I did not want Mom to see me cry.

We had an unbelievable day. Tomorrow is Sunday, our day to be together. This was a Christmas we could all learn from. We did not worry about the food, gifts, or pressures. We focused on being together. God Bless this day. Merry Christmas to all and good night.

Sunday, December 26, 2004

I feel better this morning. At the end of the day, it just got hard for me. I felt bad, but I will not apologize for my feelings.

Mom slept in this morning. Christmas Day was a big day for her. She didn't eat much today. She loves Christmas goodies, and her favorite is fudge. She keeps a small plate next her bed on her nightstand. We have a joke going. I love caramel clusters, but I can not have them since they make me sick. Mom got a box of them for Christmas from someone. It is hard for her to eat them, but she keeps them next to her bed and watches so I do not eat them. She caught me looking at them in the dining room and she let out a scream. "Bring them here! I do not trust you alone with them!" Every once in awhile, she looks to see if I have been in there._

Mom and I had a good day. We talked about what a wonderful Christmas we had. We laughed about us all being in pink. God does work through people. A few people stopped in today. Mom was glowing with the Christmas she received. We went in Mom's bedroom early in the afternoon. We watched Lifetime movies. I had to keep Mom focused so she would not lose her train of thought. Sometimes I had to bring her back into the movie. I think she enjoyed herself today. She misses watching TV. It is hard for her to stay focused enough to watch any shows now. We watched a lot of food shows tonight. She told me who her favorites were. She still remembers who they are and how to make things. She loves talking about cooking. It has to be hard talking about food and not being able to eat, but it doesn't seem to bother her.

We both have always loved reading. It is our thing that we do at the end of the day. She used to love to read her daily paper, and now she just holds it and falls asleep. She wanted the paper tonight to read. I told her it was in the dumpster. She wanted, it and we got to giggling. I told her

Living for the Moment

I was not going to go in the dumpster and get the paper for her when she would not be reading it any way. Up the index finger came. "I'm your mother, go!" she demanded. I went to obey my mother's orders. I was laughing, and I could hear her giggling in the bedroom. It had been thrown away in the morning, so I had a lot of garbage to go through. I came back in the bedroom with the prized paper to the waiting patient with a smile on her face. "I knew you would come through." She hung onto her paper as she tried to read one article at a time. We both knew she could not read a single line. It was all about living for the moment. We went to bed early.

Monday, December 27, 2004

I will be staying the whole shift today. Jeremy's grandfather passed away so Darcy needs to be with her family. I don't have anything planned. Mike, Josh and Lance will take care of the business. I'm thanking God for not bringing us any snow right now. I can spend this time with Mom.

She has some handheld slot machines, and she is acting like she's playing for real money. She is having a good time today. If only she could make one last trip to a casino, but we know that is impossible. Time moves on.

She had a lot of company today. We were serving leftover oyster stew. "It feels so good not to be dying yet. I want to have some more fun," Mom admitted to us today. We all tease her that it will take God awhile to get her room ready because he needs to be prepared for her.

Mom had a lot of energy today. Her medications are working out well, but her mind is slipping some. You have to help her finish her sentences at times. It is hard to say how much longer. I just know this time is precious time. At times we have gone from her being down in bed and saying this is it, only a few days left, she may be gone soon, to her cooking in the kitchen for herself or someone else. We should never question when it is our time. Each month I have to step up my feelings. When taking care of her, I need to keep her as my patient. That is the only way I can do my shifts. When I let my guard down, I get myself into trouble. Someday she will be my full-time Mom again. This has been a learning experience for me. In this situation, I'm amazed at

45

Brenda Ann Rebelein

what I can do. I know in the future I will have to do things I have no experience in, but it is about my patient, Marvel.

Tuesday, December 28, 2004

I stayed home today and cleaned my house and got my Christmas tree down and put the decorations back in their place. I came for the night shift. Mom went to bed at 7:00.

Wednesday, December 29, 2004

Mom, Jeanette, and I were having coffee this morning. We were talking about the past and the future. Jeanette and I are grateful for the helpful advice Mom has given us over the years. Of course, Mom would take no credit for it. "Your answer is always right in front of you," she said. We started to shed a few tears, but Mom told us to stop. "Tears are for sad times." Jeanette asked what we were going to do without Mom. Mom looked around, smiled, and said, "You will have Brenda to replace me. Is she any good? No, not really, but she'll have to do." We giggled through the tears. When the woman from hospice came to give Mom her bath, we told her she could come in if she drank coffee, ate cinnamon rolls, and shed a few tears with us. That's all Mom would allow.

Mom did have her bath today, and the bedding was changed. She is still having a bath three times a week. They will come every day when they need to. She is very tired this morning. At times we all think she is doing better then we are. Mom was antsy by the end of the day today. She wants control of her own medication, and we know that is not going to happen. I'm home for the rest of the night.

Thursday, December 30, 2004

Mom is doing well today. She is still staying in bed a little longer in the mornings. She is fighting with this rash she gets under her breasts. The itching is under control for now.

She slept all night last night. That was the third night in a row for her. She has lost so much weight, about lost 60 pounds. It is like she's melting away. She looks weaker and is unsure of herself when she walks. She's still keeping herself clean, does her hair and her makeup. She

Living for the Moment

loves when someone comes to rub her feet. Even the grandchildren get the chance to rub Grandma's feet.

I'm tired today. I know I need to keep going. It is not about me right now. I need to stay strong. I can do this. It is time to switch roles. She has always been there for me. I will not leave her, but I am going home for the night since Darcy is here.

Friday, December 31, 2004

I relieved Darcy this morning. Mom screamed in the middle of the night about a fire. She thought Mike was standing over her bed trying to help her. The rash is doing better. She has a routine now. She gets up and freshens up and then goes back to bed. She wants to be ready in case someone comes over.

We are supposed to have a good snowstorm this weekend. Mom is tired today. She is sleeping a lot more now. Sometimes she just sleeps in her chair in the dining room. Sleeping more is one of the changes we are looking for. I noticed that Mom is not taking extra pain pills during the day like she was. They have her pain under control for now.

Mom had a hard time swallowing her pills today. It was scary, but they finally went down. We have been putting them in pudding or applesauce. It makes them go down so much easier. Her biggest fear is choking to death. I keep reassuring her that the hospice nurse thinks she will just pass away. She has been praying to God that when he calls her name she will go safely.

Darcy, Jeremy, Jade and Megan stayed with Mom for New Year's Eve. They had a wonderful meal of lobster, rib eye steak, fish, herb mashed potatoes and asparagus with cheese sauce. It was the greatest thing they could have done for Mom and themselves. They had a good time. It was a wonderful way to bring in the New Year.

It is late at night, and I can not sleep. This happens a lot at night. I know I do not give my mind a rest. I have so many mixed feelings. I'm so tired emotionally. I try not to think of my needs right now. We caretakers need to take care of ourselves, but this has been a hard one for me. We have had a trying year. We pray we can keep Mom in her own home, and there are days that I hope and think that this will be possible. Things happen for a reason. I count all the blessings Mom had this year. We got to celebrate Mom's last birthday, she got to go to Las

47

Brenda Ann Rebelein

Vegas, and she went on casino trips in Chuck and Thelma's camper. I took a medical leave of absence from my waitress job right before Mom received her news. Mom talked us into buying a camper to take some time off, just for us to get away from work. We had Thanksgiving and Christmas together with the family. Mom got to end this year eating lobster. Swallowing her supper was a blessing for her. She called me to tease me. Lobster is my favorite also.

We do not know what this next year will bring, but we will be ready to face it head on. Our heads will be held up high. We pray to God that it will be His wish to keep Mom at home. She wanted to return home for her final moments. She wants us to remember how she lived, not how she died. God wants us to wait a little longer. He wants us to enjoy what He has given us. We thank Him every day for the wonderful role model He has given us in our mom and grandma, Marvel Mae.

Happy New Year, Everyone.

Chapter 4

Yesterday Is Gone and Tomorrow Is Not Here, So Let's Enjoy Today

January 2005

We are facing the fifth month in our cancer journey. We have made it through 2004, and we are all ready to face 2005 as Marvel's caretakers. I live with no regrets. My family is who I have to thank from the bottom of my heart. Mike, Josh, and Lance are working the business so I can have my time with Mom. They have always been so understanding. Monica, Desiree, and Destiny have been my lifelines, always cheering me up or giving me a hug. Lance and Kristine talk with me on the phone. People spend hours with us just to help us through the day or help with errands. The caretakers are a blessing. It takes special people to do this job.

I pray every day, and God listens to what I have to say. I want to add a prayer each day to my journal. Things are making another turn. I'm so happy God gives me the words to write in my journal. This is my place to open my world up. Everyone has his or her own way to deal with situations, but I find warmth in writing.

Saturday, January 1, 2005

Dear God, I see Mom is getting weaker and more confused. I know You are watching over us twenty-four hours a day. I can feel that You need me when I pray so hard. Last night You saw I was so tired and weak. You gave me rest. It is hard for Mom to stay awake long periods of time. Is this your sign that I've been waiting for, God? Please give me strength. I will keep the faith You have given me.

I'm here at Mom's for the day shift. She's sleeping a lot like yesterday. She is very confused at times. She told me she wants me to get some thank-you cards ready for when she passes away. She wants to thank the many people that have been a great help to her during this time. She says she is failing and she can tell. I let her talk about it. She has

Brenda Ann Rebelein

a bump on the back of her head which she says really hurts. I try to reassure her that it is nothing. We have been putting ice on it all day which seems to be helping.

The nurse will be coming soon to look at it. I need to get Mom out of her bed and into her wheelchair. She has been in her bedroom a lot more now. We take her to the bathroom and then back to the bedroom, or sometimes it so much easier to use the commode next to her bed. I still take her out in the dining room in the wheelchair so she can enjoy sitting next to the big window over the lake. Even if it is wintertime, she loves watching the kids play in the snow. It's good for her to be out of the bedroom for a few minutes.

I want to shed a few tears for her, but I know it is not time. I need to be strong right now so I can take care of Mom. I feel that if I go down, I may not get up. We have Mom's church picture on the dining room table with a candle that burns all the time. When it is time for me to take care of Mom, I stare hard at that picture. She looks so strong and beautiful in it, so in control of her life, and she has changed so much, but I want to remember her like she was before, just like she wants to be remembered.

Mom is not running to the bathroom anymore to fix her hair or put on make-up. It is all too much work for her now. Some days I bring a mirror to her bed when she is in the mood. She looks so pale and old. She is passing away in front of us, and there is nothing we can do but love her and take care of her. It has helped me to deal with this by looking at her picture because then I'm ready to take care of my patient, Marvel. Mom will always be the most beautiful person to me. I feel all of us caretakers are doing an awesome job. We all have our own way of doing things, and whatever works for each of us is what makes us all so special to do this job. I do have to hold my head up proud. I never thought I could do a lot of things that I have been doing. I did not think I was capable of this. You will do a lot of things when someone is counting on you.

Chuck and Bruce are doing well. Bruce is here during the day, Chuck in here at nights. I feel not a lot of men would take care of their Mom like these two have. They have just stepped up to the plate. Mom is proud of us and the way we have put up the schedule, brought food in, and did what was needed to be done. We will be taking baby steps as we see what is given to us. One good thing is that we have formed a team.

Mom slept all day today. The nurse was here. The bump on Mom's head is nothing to worry about. She was too weak to hold a conversation. She just wanted to rest. She did get up and have some chicken broth.

Mom's friends from Arizona stopped in. They are headed back home. It was tough on all three of them, knowing that this is the last time they will see each other. They have been friends for many years. It was emotional, and I left the room so they could have their time alone for their final good-bye. They hugged and thanked her for all she had done for them all their lives. I was called back in the room, of course. I was the coffee and dessert server. Mom always has to lighten up the mood. "Do you have any New Year's resolution, Marvel?" they had asked her.

"Yes, I do," she said. "To be happy the last few days I have left and have a painless death." They visited a little more and talked about the good old days. Mom just wanted to enjoy their moments laughing about the dumb things they use to do. It was so hard for Mom when they left. They were some of her best friends. She wanted to talk and share her feelings on how much it hurts to know you will never see them again until they meet you in heaven.

She was tired, and I helped her back in bed. She wanted to be alone to rest. The rest of the day she slept well. God bless her for being so positive and strong. She is always cheering us up, telling us the good things we should be looking at. I got to go home for the night.

Sunday, January 2, 2005

Dear God, I always feel You near me. You hear my prayers. I felt You near me when I got home. I prayed to You hard and loud tonight. You have answered my prayers. You saw me getting tired, so You picked me up and carried me and had me rest. Sleep is hard to come by at times. I know You came down and put your hands on Mom's head. She has taken a turn for the worse in the last three days. She was so determined to walk with her wheelchair, but her legs were so weak. You have her resting comfortably in bed. We were so afraid she would fall. Dear God, watch over us all. Give me the strength and wisdom I need. I need You, as I cannot walk through this alone. I will try to be patient while we take this journey. God, be with me as I face another day.

Mom is having a bad day. She is so weak and can only hold small conversations. She was saying things that I have not said. It is easier just to agree. Does it matter who is right or wrong? I have learned how to talk around things so Mom will not get upset. She is lying in bed listening to the church service on the radio as she does every Sunday morning. Then we listen to her three funeral songs. We never get sick of hearing them. I hope we do not wear the music out before the funeral. It breaks my heart when Mom is so still. We cannot have her up cooking anymore.

Now there is a change of plans. She wants some soup and garlic toast. I pray she can swallow this.

She did just fine. We just got done painting her fingernails and toenails, and now she is reading her horoscope which tells her to take care of all unfinished business. She is laughing hard. "My only business is to die. How do you die when you don't die, for dumb." She thinks this is so funny. She calls Chuck at home, but he does not think this is as funny as we do. I cannot help from laughing. She is so happy tonight, like her old self at times. Mom and I have had humor throughout this experience. It seems to help us each day. Mom is right. Why be sad? We are lucky we have had this time. You might as well enjoy yourself as much as you can. She calls Sheila from next door and orders a chili hotdog with extra cheese and onions. Sheila delivers this to her bedside with a smile. Each day this woman surprises us.

Mom ended up having a good day. She wanted her favorite meal: fried chicken, mashed potatoes with gravy, and stewed tomatoes. While she was talking about her meal and how to cook it, she slowly fell asleep for the night.

Monday, January 3, 2005

Dear God, Mom is having a lot of pain in the back of her head. I have been icing it to help with the pain. At times I'm so scared. Hear my prayer. Let me feel Your arms around me today. I will be the caretaker for the day. Hear my prayer.

Mom is still having a lot of pain in the back of her head. I have been sitting near her head. She does not want to go far. I think we are both scared today. I try to let her think that there is nothing to worry

Living for the Moment

about. Like my girlfriend's son tells her, "You are worrying more than you are praying."

Mom still loves listening to her music at night. Late at night, every night, they play Mom and Dad's favorite song, "Sentimental Journey." She wakes up every time it is on.

The hospice nurse and bath lady were here today. Mom feels so much better when she has a bath and clean bedding on the bed. She has been sleeping now for awhile. I have to go home and help Mike with the business. I promised myself I would take care of me today. I need some time in my own home. It is like getting refueled so I can keep taking care of Mom.

Tuesday, January 4, 2005

Dear God, I'm so grateful for my surroundings in my home. Today was a good day for me to just look around my home. I'm grateful for what I have, not what I want. I'm so blessed to have a wonderful family and a beautiful home. Today is a good day for counting my blessings.

I got called to stay with Mom for the rest of the day. Once again, Mike and Josh took over my share of work in the business with no questions asked. Today there was no bath lady and no nurse, so it was nice for Mom to get to sleep in and not have to get up. It was nice to have a laid back day. She slept off and on all day. She was light on her feet, though, and she lost her balance a lot today. I was walking close to her to catch her when she was ready to fall. It ended up being a very stressful day. She would try to lie down, and then she would be up again right away. There was no place to go but back and forth to the dining room.

Mom will not settle down. She has been talking about cooking something good. I know I cannot have her in the kitchen working. Then she was messing with the things she had on her nightstand, for hours moving things around and cleaning things out. She was not hurting anything. I can see the cancer is taking over Mom more and more each day. Her quality of life seems to be slipping away.

Mom was getting very antsy, and she refused to take her medication. She was getting mean about it. I didn't know what to do, and everyone was working, so I had no one to call for help. I quietly called a friend.

53

Brenda Ann Rebelein

I asked this earth angel to pretend she was a person who Mom loves and trusts to help her take her medication. "Mom, you are wanted on the phone."

She eagerly grabbed the phone away from me. "Hello. Who is this?" My earth angel told Mom she was her friend.

"Marvel you need to take your medication for your daughter. She is trying to help you."

Mom listened so intently and said, "Okay I will."

"You take your medication, and I will stay on the line until you do, so you do it."

Mom opened her mouth really wide. "Okay, I did it. I took my medication." They said good-bye as I sighed with relief. I thanked my earth angel and we hung up. Mom is always breaking the mold somewhere. I was so grateful for having someone on the other end of the phone as I was so powerless. I cannot say enough words for friends and family. What they have done for our family is priceless. They will do anything to make this journey so much easier for us. We are so lucky to have them. Hospice is always a call away, twenty-four hours a day.

Dear God, I finally have Mom resting now. God, watch over us caretakers. I love my Mom, but my stress level is running high. Today was a tough one. I know tomorrow will be better. Tomorrow is a new day. Help me look for the good things. Dear Lord, I need to give You the control. This is too big for me to handle alone.

Wednesday, January 5, 2005

Dear God, I thank You for the 4 ½ inches of snow You sent me. I know You knew I needed a break from the situation at Mom's. I will go back with a new outlook when I get done working. I called a friend of Mom's to stay the day with her. I will work with Mike moving snow. I pray for our safety as I work along side my family. Thank You for taking control of my life.

Mom had her bath today. They said she was restless more than usual. This was nothing that they could not handle. Family and friends are great to have close to us right now. I do not know what we would do without those that have helped us out. Mom finally did settle down, but it took until bedtime.

54

Living for the Moment

Thursday, January 6, 2005

Dear God, thank You for the snow. You saw I was getting tired and needed a break. You held my hand and carried me away from the situation. I feel refreshed and ready to go again. I can walk once again. I know you will carry me when you feel I need it.

I worked with Mike today. It is good being at work. I miss it so much. Mom called me and forgot what she had called for. She knows that I have to work. I spend so much time there; I think she gets use to me being there so much. She said she misses my caretaking. I told her she tells that to everybody. She was confused on the phone at times. I told her I would call her later when we got done working.

I called Mom when we got done working. She was having lots of company. She was laughing that she must be boring for her company because she keeps falling asleep. It is amazing how one woman can have so much company. She has a big heart for a lot of people. They can now pay her back when they come to see her. Mom's door has always been open. She was talking to people in the middle of the night. She said they were in her room. It can be long nights for the caretakers when she's restless.

Friday, January 7, 2005

Dear God, thank You for giving the granddaughters time with their grandma last night as they were taking care of her. It will always be a time they will remember. It does not matter if they stay, call on the phone, or stop in to say hi. It always makes Mom smile and makes her day better. Grandma is special to them. It helps make memories and keeps them warm at night. You have given us time to prepare ourselves. I feel You have taught Mom how to prepare us for her death. Grandchildren are loved.

I did not have to go to Mom's until the night shift. That helped me get caught up on a few things at home. I feel refreshed and ready for another shift. Mom and I had a quiet night tonight. She is so much more relaxed since they changed her medication. We spent the night in her bedroom talking about what it will be like without her. She went down the list of each member of the family. She talked about what she liked about them and where she thought they would be years from now. She is so proud of her family. She is a very positive lady.

55

She talked about how she was looking for Dad last night and could not find him. "He can only hide so long and I will find him." She smiled then and talked about how they met. Mom wanted me to reassure her that when the time gets tough, her kids will be by her bedside. I held her hand and told her that we are a team and of course we will be there. It was a quiet night.

Saturday, January 8, 2005

Dear God, watch over Mom and her caretakers today. I will take a day off for me. I'm glad she is resting and more comfortable. I may go and buy myself some new clothes. You made women for shopping.

It gets harder to leave Mom each day. I know I need to take care of myself. That has been a hard one for me to learn. I know it is getting to be more work taking care of Mom. I know there will be a day soon that I will not get to go there and take care of her or just to stop in and say hi.

Mom slept all day.

Sunday, January 9, 2005

Dear God, I thank You for each day with Mom. I do love Sundays the best. We listen to the church services, and then we listen to her funeral music. Then we always have a lot of company on Sundays. These days will keep me warm forever.

Today was a different day. We did not have much company. It gave her time to sleep more. She is sleeping off and on all day in her chair or in bed. She can fall asleep so quickly. We spend a lot more time in her bedroom now that we've convinced her that people do not mind coming in there to see her. She loves her funeral music: "A Friend We Have in Jesus," "One Day at a Time," and "Dark Clouds." She talked about her funeral to make sure everything is ready. She drew a picture of what her flowers would look like. There will be forty-two carnations in a tall L-shape representing one for each member of the family and a big white candle in the middle with her church picture in it. She can relax knowing she is getting everything she wanted.

She was sliding down in bed. I had to pull her up, but she helped with the heels of her feet. Boy, did she fly. She called me a bull. We had some laughs tonight. When I gave her a dose of medicine in some strawberry applesauce that she didn't like, I told her she had to swallow it anyway because it had her medicine in it and I was the only caretaker for the evening. She asked me when my shift was over because she didn't like me, but she said it with a smile. It makes the night go faster to joke around like that. She slept well again tonight.

Monday, January 10, 2005

Dear God, give me strength each day when I leave Mom. I never know what kind of shape she will be in when I come back the next time. I have some strength as we take this unknown journey together.

It is hard for Mom to stay focused on a conversation. Sometimes you can see she is battling with this. She told me today that people have to know she is slipping. Her wisdom is all used up. They will have to deal with their own and have faith in themselves that they can make it and do well.

She was in bed early. She was tired and not feeling well. She is getting really weak again, but she bounces back so much you never know about this lady. When Mom passes away, I should not feel bad. Yes, I will miss her, but she has no quality of life anymore like she said today. She also told me today that she has had a great life and is ready to move on. We will wait and see what God has in store for us.

Tuesday, January 11, 2005

Dear God, we received the snow you ordered for us. I'm grateful for Jeanette and Darcy for taking care of my shifts at Mom's. It was peaceful moving snow. My mind can just wonder, and I do not have to think about checking on Mom, medication times, or all the things that go with it. It is nice giving the mind a break. I'm blessed to have a job to go to and one I can work around when I want to work. I pray for all our family and friends.

I was suppose to be at Mom's tonight for my shift, but the snowstorm coming in called for a change of plans. I called Mom two times, and she called me two times. Phone calls were our thing, and we were always getting into trouble with all the phone calls we had in a month. She is slipping more each day. We miss each other when we are apart,

57

Brenda Ann Rebelein

and I'm sure everyone else feels the same way. Also, Mom can boss me around, as she knows I will do anything she says. I do a lot of shifts at Mom's.

I will get there when I can. For now we have to focus on cleaning up this snow with all the businesses we have. It also gives other people time to be with her. At times it is hard to find a replacement with everyone working.

Her medication is working well right now. Her mind is slower, and she never gets out of the "being tired" mode. For now I will take her any way I can get her. Soon I will be going to the cemetery to have my time with her. I'm just not ready for that yet.

She had a good day. I was glad to hear that. It is hard for me when she is having a hard day and I cannot be there. I know I cannot stop it. It is just being there that makes me feel better.

I forgot to write this in my journal on Sunday afternoon. We were watching some cooking shows together in Mom's bedroom. She has her favorite cooks, and then she has some that she thinks should go back to school. She tells me if she agrees with what they are cooking. They were making all these fancy meals. We looked at each other. It was making us hungry. Because Mom is only eating a few bites of food at a time now, we do not eat in front of her or cook in the house because of the smells. It is not fair to her when she cannot eat. We bring food already prepared into the house. We are blending her food in a mixer now; it is the only way she can swallow. We got hungry, so I went and got her three bites of corn flakes and myself some cheerios, and we had a meal in her bedroom as we finished watching the cooking shows. It was the best meal I think I have ever had.

Mom and I like to talk about what we think heaven is like. Everyone has his or her own thoughts on that one. She gave me another talk about being strong. I know she is helping me prepare for her death. I had to promise her I would not overwork myself. She thinks that I work too hard.

She taught me what I know. I know we get along because I tell her what I know she wants to hear. Then she seems to relax more. She is teaching me to have the strength to face each day, that everything happens for a reason, and that I should never question it, but just accept

58

Living for the Moment

it for what it is. We are doing one day at a time and some days even less than that.

The snow is still falling. We will have a lot of cleanup.

Wednesday, January 12, 2005

Dear God, I had to cancel going to Mom's. We are still getting snow. Keep her safe for the day as You watch over her and her caretakers. I'm so grateful for the nurses and the staff of hospice for all the wonderful care they are giving Mom. This would not be possible if we did not have this large group of people coming together to take care of her. It is a bond you will not find anywhere else.

It was a busy morning this morning. Mom called me a few times. She loves calling the hospice office every day. She makes up excuses to call them. I think she just likes to call and talk to them. We can see Mom's mind is slipping more and more each day. Darcy and I have talked about how she would feel if she really knew what was going on. Some of things she does or says are out of her control. It is the disease, not Mom. She always had plans to live until she was in her nineties like her mom. She is only seventy-seven. God had other plans for her. She has accepted this cancer news with such pride and dignity. When someone is here, it is not about her. She asks them about their family and things they like to do.

I'm really proud of my daughter, Monica. No matter how busy she is, she calls Mom every day. Mom loves phone calls. They are just as important as visits. Sheila's family stops in every day. Vicki, Miranda and Aurora stop in with the kids. It is a good feeling when she knows people are thinking of her. Mom's grandchildren come when they can, or they call her. With it being a big family, someone is always stopping in to say "hi" or crawling up in bed with Grandma to give her a hug or two.

There is a new change of plans. I got a call from Mom's. She is very antsy and hard to handle. She will not stay put for very long. She is weak on her feet, and it is very easy for her to fall. She has been good about using the wheelchair, but sometimes she walks away from her walker. I sometimes let out a yell, and she laughs. She wants to cook for everyone that is coming to her house, but she is only eating a few bites. She says everyone else has to eat. I told Jeanette I would give

59

Brenda Ann Rebelein

her another anxiety pill and see how that goes. She has another bad hangnail on her toe, and she wanted me to come and fix it now right away; this could not wait. I told her I was moving snow, and I would get there as soon as I could.

When I got to Mom's, things had settled down for Jeanette. I had some selfish thoughts tonight before I left home. I would have loved to throw on some pajamas and snuggle up to a good book. I do have a few pairs of pajamas left at home. Mom has wanted me to keep all the others for her to wear. I have never been crabby through this whole journey, but I was tonight. I guess we all have our moments. The stress we are all living under seems unbearable at times. I just cannot think about it. I just have to move on and do what I need to do.

Mom was comfortable tonight. Those anxiety pills do work. We got the bad hangnail out of her toe with Anbesol. We think that if it is good enough for your mouth, it has to be good enough for your toes.

Mom still sleeps off and on in her chair. It helped when hospice told her she should take a little catnap where she is. She needs her rest when she is tired. It was like Mom needed the okay.

I love to read. It is a good pastime for me when Mom is sleeping.

She woke up again. She was laughing about how she can be talking and holding a conversation and then quickly falls asleep. "How dumb this is," she said. "Let's go to the bedroom since we have no company." She wanted me to stay next to her bed in the chair in case she needed something, then I would be near her.

Mom's birthday is March 16. We all go to the casino in Morton for her birthday to celebrate. She was laughing as she thought about possibly making it to her party. She made it to Thanksgiving, Thelma's birthday party, and Christmas, and now we are facing her birthday. Who would have thought she would have so much fun in the little time she had left.

Once I got Mom settled in bed, she told me we needed to talk. "It's about my birthday. I do not think I will make it there. We need to be honest. We both know that I'm slipping. But you kids will all go and have a good time there for my birthday. I will find someone to hire to stay with me for the weekend to take care of me. Nothing will stand in the way of my birthday plans. I know truthfully that I will not be going. And who knows, maybe I will be smiling from up above." I looked at

60

her sadly, knowing I would never leave her at home with someone else. She knew what I was thinking. Up came the index finger as it always does when she means business. "Stop it. I do not want to hear another thing about it. You all go and have a good time. No matter what, you do not cancel our reservations," Mom demanded.

What a remarkable women lies next to me. She is our angel on this earth. To think of life without her is unbearable right now. She is the rock of this family. I told her that she needs to send us a sign when she gets to heaven safely. Maybe that is what we are all nervous about. I need to stop and smell the roses today. I was getting a little excited earlier. Slow down, Brenda, just for today.

Thursday, January 13, 2005

Dear God, thank you for sending me where I need to be. There is so much going on in my life. I'm going from my house to Mom's and doing the things that need to be done. There is nothing better than going to a place I have called home. I'm grateful You have given us all this time to build new memories.

Mom slept well last night. She looks good this morning. Things go well when she is well-rested. She got up and insisted on making a small stack of pancakes. I walked close by her, but she does okay as long as she uses her walker. I have to give a yell once in awhile. "You're forgetting something," I'll say. Then she giggles as she tries to leave without it.

How can one woman make such a big mess for pancakes? She was so proud and happy that she could cook in her kitchen once again, but eating is another story? She had three bites and was done. She thinks it is funny she can have as much syrup and butter as she wants because she doesn't have to watch her weight like the rest of us. The important thing is that she was satisfied she could cook again. That's what it was really all about.

I was cleaning up her mess in the kitchen when I heard her say, "Look, Mommy, no hands." She was walking from her dining room chair to her sitting chair with no walker and her hands up in the air. She was counting out loud but taking slow, small steps. She laughed as she sat down. She doesn't realize she could fall and get hurt, and then she would not get to stay in her own home. I was angry and nervous at

61

Brenda Ann Rebelein

first, but she was laughed and told me, "I know I should have not done it, but it gets boring around here. I wanted to see if I could do it."

She tried to read the paper. "I'm going to go and start some laundry in the basement. Do you think that you can behave for those few minutes?" I asked her.

She was hiding behind her paper, giggling. "Of course honey," she said. I hurried as fast as I could because now I don't know how much I can trust her to be alone. When I came up from the basement, I could hear her giggling. She was walking back to her chair without her walker again. She was trying to see if she could get from the table to her chair and back again before I got back from the basement and caught her. She laughed so hard, I knew then I would not trust her the rest of the day to be alone even for a few minutes. It's at times like this I do not know if it is the drugs or just Mom being Mom.

I noticed she has more purple marks on her arms and legs. I know that is one thing that I should be watching for. She has a small one on her face. I hope she doesn't notice. She loves her face being perfect.

Each day we are given is so precious. At times it is like I'm walking around in slow motion, even though my life is a rat race from working, getting things done, or quick-packing a bag for the next shift at Mom's, even though I might have as much stuff in her house by now as she does.

Mom and I had some fun today. We rolled up newspaper and got two small waste paper baskets and played paper basketball. It was fun, and we laughed a lot. We hope no one saw us doing this. They would think we had lost it or that we are spending too much time together. Mom called a few neighbors and family members to see if they wanted to join us. Who knows what they were thinking? We did end up getting some company, and we had the whole dining room full of rolled up newspaper from missed baskets. I let her win, but only because my basket was full.

Mom's medication seems to be working well. When things get rocky, we give her an anxiety pill. I wonder if at times she has pain but doesn't know it or think to say anything. We are also giving her extra anxiety medication at bedtime. It helps her sleep through the night. Her mind seems to be slipping, but physically she seems to be getting stronger. They say they have one big burst of energy before they pass away. We've had to laugh because Mom has had so many. She is the first in a lot of things hospice has never seen before. That would be our mom and grandma.

We always have a lot of questions for hospice every time they come here. There is never a stupid question, they say. Her blood pressure has gone down a little. She just keeps surprising us all the time. We keep saying that Mom is doing better than her caretakers.

Friday, January, 14, 2005

Dear God, I will be home for the day and night unless something changes. Please give Mom and her caretakers a good day. This experience is making us all stronger as a family. Our friends are just as important. They are always a call away. Each day is a gift and a blessing.

It is nice being at home. I really miss being here. Mom was good this morning, but then she wanted control over her medication again. She finally settled down at suppertime.

She is sipping on malts that people bring her. We keep extra malts in the freezer for her. She's only eating a few bites now and then. She will eat my waffles. She fills them up with lots of butter and syrup to help them slide down. We are putting her medication in applesauce or pudding. It is easier for her to swallow, plus then she doesn't question what each pill is.

It was very cold out tonight, but Mom stayed in bed where it is nice and warm. When I was there this morning, her feet and legs were really blue and swollen. We all know that is a sign. Hospice helps me to understand this terrible disease that is controlling our lives.

It is nice when the grandchildren help take shifts on Friday nights. But, of course, Mom loves it just as much as they do.

God, please watch over me. Sometimes I get so scared. I will not lose my faith.

Saturday, January 15, 2005

Dear God, I see Mom is slipping more and more all the time. I need to learn to enjoy what time we have left. I will accept and follow where You lead me. Please put Your hand on her head. Give her encouragement and guidance on her final journey. I feel You near me at the beginning of each day. If I pray right, it only takes one prayer

Brenda Ann Rebelein

a day, as we live one day at a time. We are living for each moment. My faith has never been as strong as it is now. I have learned so much on this cancer journey. You have given me the wisdom to learn.

I was home for the day. Chuck said Mom was in bed all day today. I needed this day at home. It will help me get refreshed for starting another week at Mom's.

Sunday, January 16, 2005

Dear God, You see Mom and I are tired today. Please carry us at this point of our journey. She is sleeping a lot more. It is hard for her to stay awake. You have her sleeping comfortably, but I'm emotionally drained. God, hear my prayer.

Today is Sunday, when Mom and I spend the whole day together. She has slept all day.

I've been feeling that it's time for me to strengthen my emotions so I can handle what is in store for us next.

For supper she wanted a hard egg, very burnt bacon, and toast. While I was making it, I knew she wouldn't eat it, but then, you never know. She is always surprising us. She just pushed it away and apologized for being a nuisance.

She was trying to read the newspaper and kept falling asleep. Her head fell down hard and fast. I thought for a moment that she had passed away. I told her I was tired. "Let's get more comfortable in bed." She agreed. She can't have an electric blanket anymore with her oxygen tank, so today I brought her a warm comforter. She is always cold.

Today Mom looks so old and frail, but I will always remember my hero, protector, role model, and mother. She has taught us to be the best we can be. When we did not have faith in ourselves, she taught us to find the courage we needed to make it through.

She didn't have much company today. This was an unusual Sunday.

Monday, January 17, 2005

Dear God, I know You are listening this morning. I keep seeing more changes in Mom. Hear my prayer. I will learn more patience as we go through this together.

Living for the Moment

This morning was a tough one. When my shift was over, I went to give Mom a hug and kiss as I do every time I leave. She cried so hard that she shook. She wanted me to stay, but I knew I had to go to work. It broke my heart as she cried in my arms so hard. "When you kids leave, I never know if this is the last time I will see you. I just want to enjoy every moment. I know the time is getting closer and that I do not have much time left. Please stay."

I had some commitments for the day. I knew I had to leave. "I'm sorry, Mom. I will get back as soon as I can. I love you." I knew I had to pull myself away or I would never leave. It was hard leaving her when I could hear her crying. I rushed out the door and could not look back.

Seeing her so upset does something to me. She has always been a woman who has been in control of herself. I feel so powerless in this situation. She has pleaded with us to have no tears. Now that things are moving along, she is losing control, and her tears prove this. It was like she was looking right through me and did not hear a thing I had said. I know this is part of the process, but it is so hard to understand, especially when you've never been through this before. It was hard holding my head up and walking out that door and then going to a customer's house and smiling and doing the best job I can. I always say to myself. "What would Mom do?" That has helped me a lot.

I called later, and she had the nurse and the bath lady there. Then she wanted to be left alone for the day. She had lots of company in the late afternoon. That got her out of her bedroom for awhile. She did not talk much but just smiled and listened to everyone else talk. She went to bed early. Jeanette had the day shift, and Darcy had the night shift.

Tuesday, January 18, 2005

Dear God, I feel You near me while I sit near Mom's bed. You have given both of us some peace and comfort today. Thank you for the last few months of togetherness we have had and the memories that will live with us forever. So many people do not get this experience, to keep their loved ones at home. I still feel You are carrying us each day. I do not feel powerless today. I have the faith that You will guide me to our future.

Mom is sleeping through the nights once in awhile. When she gets up, it is to use the bathroom. Then she goes right back to bed. There

65

Brenda Ann Rebelein

haven't been any bad fire dreams in a long time. When she woke up, she wanted some warm tea. She had some sips and then went right back to sleep. She is in the sleeping mode today. The phone rings, but she doesn't move. I have been sitting by her bed all day. I love to read and write, so that keeps me busy.

It is my job right now to make Mom feel safe. Before, she would open her eyes to see if I was still sitting next to her. Now she doesn't do that anymore. I brush away the few tears that once in awhile run down her face.

My shift for the day was almost over when Mom woke from sleeping all day. I told her it was Mike's birthday today. She threw the bed covers off and wanted help in the kitchen. She was walking pretty slow and sure of herself. She had some BBQ ribs already baked in the freezer; she just added some sauce to them. I helped her put them in the oven for me to take home for him. She was happy he had a birthday supper made by her. Where does this energy come from?

She had some company; and we had pie and ice cream. Jeanette is always giving us baked goods. Sitting, reading, and eating are just what I need.

I had to stay a little longer today. Mom was in bed the rest of the day after her company left. She said she's starting to get scared a little. She is having a hard time swallowing her food. Our special joke is that waffles still go down the best. Her biggest fear is to choking to death.

She has always had good, positive faith. She believes you follow God and never question His work. We talked, and she feels it is hard for her to pray right now. I thought that maybe a person goes through this during this time. Is this normal, to have these feelings? We prayed together. We asked God to help restore her faith. She has been joking about heaven and how she will have control, but now the joking has left her. She knows the time gets closer each day. I think it is time for Pastor Soli to come and talk with Mom. I called him, and he will stop in tomorrow. Darcy has been reading the Bible to her. Her fingers and feet hurt so much. I told her it was arthritis, and she was relieved. She thought it was the cancer taking over her body. It made her feel better.

I sat next to her bed until my shift was over. She woke up once in awhile to see if I was still sitting next to her. She thanked me for staying close. She does not want to die alone. With the time moving closer to the end, it is getting harder for me to leave each time. I'm so lucky I can still see and touch her. Mike was very surprised when I came home and told him Mom had made him supper. She is a strong woman. She's still having her bursts of energy.

Wednesday, January, 19, 2005

Dear God, it is hard for Mom to pray right now. She has never lost faith before, so this has to be scary for her. Lend her a hand to show her she will be okay. Each day that comes and goes, my faith only gets stronger. I will follow the path You lead me down. You have made me so much stronger as You see I can walk alone again. I know You will carry me again when you feel the time is needed. God helps those who help themselves.

Today was an emotional day for me. I had a tough one for the books. Pastor Soli came and talked with Mom. I let them have their alone time. We have all prayed together as a family, and now I feel it is good for Mom to have her alone time. I'm tired, so I have not been sleeping well. I know I have to pick up extra hours here. Everyone is busy right now. We have to cover a lot of hours since she needs care twenty-four hours a day, seven days a week. I know what I need to do. I need to step up to the plate and get myself more emotionally ready. I'm so lucky I have the husband and the kids that I do. They are taking care of the business, keeping the house clean, and even washing clothes. They are there when I need to talk to someone.

I will try to stay positive. I will keep going forward thinking about what needs to be done. If she can lie there and be positive in this situation, so can I. Her visit with the Pastor helped. She has slept all day. When I get upset, I get on my treadmill and pretend that I'm headed miles and miles away. Sometimes I even head for another state. I get healthy while letting off steam. I know I feel better when I get there.

Mom is failing, and you can see it. She did not even know that I left tonight to go home. Mike talked to me tonight, and he can see I'm starting to turn her into Mom and not my patient anymore. My emotions are getting in the way of the care I can give her. If I'm going to spend all those hours there, I need to stay focused. I know that I'm losing control of my emotions today. It is time to get my feelings in

Brenda Ann Rebelein

check. I have made it this far being strong. I will not give up on her, my family, or myself. I will survive this. Tomorrow is a new day.

Thursday, January 20, 2005

Dear God, I'm okay again. You saw I was tired and emotionally drained. You sent Mike to help me get stronger. I will live this journey with no regrets. I will do what I have to for Mom. I need to help someone who cannot help themselves. I need to count on myself as she is counting on me. Hear my prayer of thanks.

I was at home for the whole day. It was something I needed. Mom slept all day. She is slipping really fast. Each time I go to her house, I can see the change in her. She still has the same medications. Her mind is failing, and she is not talking very much. She is so weak, and it is so nice when she is willing to use the commode next to her bed. She hates to make us work. I told her that is what we are here for, to help her and to try to make things easier for her. We take the path we should follow. God will lead the way. Mom stayed in bed into the night. She was only out of bed once today and tonight.

Friday, January 21, 2005

Dear God, I'm feeling a lot better. I have had some time to myself and that seemed to help. Mom has great caretakers. I will try not to think of things just for now. Pastor Soli and Pastor Gary stopped in to see Mom. They have brought her faith back. I'm sure her feelings are normal when in this situation. We are so grateful for their visits. It helps us just as much as it does her. I'm blessed with good faith. Everything happens for a reason.

Darcy is with Mom today. She did not get up all morning. Darcy had to wake her for her morning pills. This afternoon, the phone rang at my house. It was Mom, and her voice was like it was before she got sick. She was upbeat and wanted to know what I was doing. It was hard to find the words because she was talking like her old self. We talked about the weather. We are in the middle of a bad snowstorm. It was a shock how good she sounded. It almost took my breath away until reality set in when I hung up. With the snowstorm here, I will work until every thing is cleaned up.

68

Saturday, January 22, 2005

Dear God, please keep us safe as we work today. Watch over Mom and her caretakers as they spend the day together. Yesterday is gone, and tomorrow is not here, so let us enjoy today.

We got a lot of snow last night and today. This is going to take a long time to remove. We have a lot of customers, and we received a few extra calls. Mom has called me a few times today. It is hard working and knowing I would like to be there. But then, to survive, I know that I need time away. I can tell she is having some anxiety. She is getting ready to fry liver and onions. Chuck is with her today. She has dishes, liver, and soap all in the dishpan. Chuck quickly told me on the phone. I told him to give her what he could of the anxiety medication so she does not get too far out of hand. She cooked some liver and was satisfied and went to bed for the rest of the day. She completed her task. Chuck threw it away in the garbage.

Mom cannot make phone calls anymore on her own. We have to help her. At suppertime, she called me once again. The old mom was talking upbeat wanting to know what I was doing? I informed her that with the storm, we had a lot of snow removal to do. She gave me some advice she wanted me to think about. At the end of the conversation, she was mumbling on the phone so I could not understand what she was saying.

I did not get to Mom's until 8:30 that night. She was sleeping really well when I got there. I have not been at her house for three days. It was good being in my own home. I did get a little taste of what my old life was like before this cancer journey started. I know that I'm doing the best I can with both homes.

Sunday, January 23, 2005

Dear God, it is good to be at Mom's again. Thank you for helping me get refreshed and catch my breath because at times this is so overwhelming. This has given others their time to have with her.

Mom slept in this morning. I did not sleep well last night. She wanted the radio on. It was on so loud, so who could sleep? It was her depressing music all night long. She loves it, though, and I guess that is all that matters. This has been a joke between us. Mom and Dad's song, "Sentimental Journey," came on three times last night. Her mind is slipping. She will be talking, and then she stops and has no idea what she is talking about. She is a good actress. She is starting to forget people. She probably does not know who I am at times. She asked me when someone comes in the room to say their name so then it may come to her. She feels bad about it, but there is nothing she can do about it, and it is not her fault. Everyone will understand.

Today is Sunday. Mom had a dining room full of people. Of course, lunch was served and everyone got their favorite beverage which she keeps on hand for everyone. She kept slipping away from the conversations. It helps that everyone goes along with it. They can see she is struggling with conversations, and she would look at me to help her finish her sentence. It was hard at times. I did not know what she was trying to say. When it was time for bed, as weak as she was, she was trying to run over my toes with her walker. Then she would giggle. Her company means the world to her. She thinks how boring it would be if no one would come here. She made me promise again tonight that when things get bad, no one sees her but her kids. "It's my life."

Monday, January 24, 2005

Dear God, today is about acceptance and respecting people for who they are. Let me not be judgmental. Who am I to cast stones? I will treat others as I want to be treated. Give me strength to take care of me. With all this strength that I have been asking for, I should be very strong when this journey is over. Today is my choice what kind of day that I will have.

Today was a busy day. Mom was up early this morning. I have the day shift. She had a bath. Our hospice nurse was here. She said that Mom's blood pressure is a little low. Everything else is looking good. Mom is looking so rough. We keep telling her she looks fine to reassure her. She is not running around the house anymore like she was, unless that changes again. She is doing her hair sometimes, and make up once in awhile. That was one thing that I had always admired. No matter how sick she was, the first thing she did in the morning was go to the bathroom and do her hair and makeup.

I feel things are progressing. I know we all keep saying that. It is time now. She is looking rough. The cancer is taking its toll on her. She only has her hair fixed now when we call for an appointment.

Our bath lady said it is getting harder to get Mom in and out of the bathtub. She will be receiving her baths in bed with sponge baths. We are still listening to her funeral music. It is so beautiful, but some people do not like to listen to it. Some of us find comfort in it. A close friend is singing it and that means the world to us. It makes it more special.

We had a big day today. She had a lot of company. She sat in her chair in the dining room a long time. It was hard for her to get up. She was very weak and tired. She went and had a nice nap, and that gave me time to get caught up on the dishes and the laundry. We are always serving lunch or desert every day. It was a hard day for me, but a nice one for her. When her company was here, she was so lost in the conversations that I could not keep up with her.

She was staring outside a lot today. She loves her big deck window. There is an opening in the ice so she can watch the geese every day that she is out of bed. This is when my heart goes out to her. Enjoy these moments.

Tuesday January 25, 2005

Dear God, I'm feeling selfish right now. Please help me turn my selfishness into gratuity. I miss my old life. Help me receive this turn my life has taken. I will be grateful for what I have now. Count my blessings. There is a lot there. I have a lot to share with others. It is better to give than to receive.

Today was another tough one at Mom's. Jeanette was the caretaker. Mom was having a lot of anxiety. She would not stay put and wanted to go in the kitchen, but she is not strong enough anymore for that. We do not want her to get hurt. She knows she wants to cook, but she cannot think what to do anymore. We have always said that if she died in the kitchen, she would be a happy lady. She is very confused today and is having a hard time with walking and has no strength in her arms. Jeanette was having a hard time calming her down. She was sleeping by the time that my shift started. She slept a couple of hours. Then she was ready to go again. She could not get up alone. She was

Brenda Ann Rebelein

calm and relaxed. She called four people to get her groceries. We had an uneventful night after that.

Wednesday, January 26, 2005

Dear God, today I need to slow my feelings down. It is hard for me not to ask, Where do we go from here? I keep thinking of the future. It is time for me to enjoy the moment and not worry about the tomorrows. I'm worrying more than I'm praying. I will try to do a better job. God, let Mom feel You near her as I do.

I prayed for a better day for Jeanette and Mom. God does answer prayers. They had a good day. Mom was calm and wanted to sleep. I do the night shift tonight. We are still running the shifts from eight in the morning to five at night and five at night to eight in the morning. This works out for everyone. We have a few people we can call to come in for a few hours if someone has to leave early and the others cannot get there in time. It is always good to have a good back-up crew.

I have really been seeing physical decline in Mom's cancer journey. Everyone can see how she is starting to fail. The hospice nurse was here and can see the changes. This is the first time they have ever said anything like that. They talked about how she is the first in different things they have ever seen before. Let it be our mom and grandma to break the mold.

Mom is a lot weaker. She needs a lot more help with things. We have to help her in and out of bed now. Her feet are really swollen again. Her purple marks are going further up her legs than before.

When Mom woke up, she had some milk and our famous waffles. She was only up a few minutes. She knew she belonged in bed and was way too weak. She was feeling sick tonight. She feels things are starting to close in on her. She asked me to stay close to her. I see Mom's color is starting to change. She is now getting cold to the touch which is another sign to watch for. She was having some hot flashes, and for awhile, it was like she was having trouble breathing. Her breathing was raspy through the night.

Thursday, January 27, 2005

Dear God, I felt You near me last night. I did not worry, and I was not scared. You guide Mom through this cancer journey. I know You need to carry me once in

Living for the Moment

awhile when I need it. Thank you for being there for me. How do people go through this when they are not believers? I will pray for them to see the light.

I feel last night was another milestone. Mom is not walking anymore. She is shuffling to get to the bathroom. She is so weak. I hang onto her because I do not want her to fall. They have given us a safety belt for her, so she will have to use that if she stays this weak. She is so confused, and she's not making conversation much anymore. She just wants to rest. I sat next to her bed last night. She would open her eyes and look at me and smile and say, "Thanks for staying close."

Last night Monica and Desiree and Destiny came to see us. Monica talked about how they need to use their inside voices. They went into Mom's room so nice and quiet, like little mice. Mom smiled. She glows when the little ones come to see her. Destiny is three years-old and says in a real loud voice, "Grandma, I'm here. Get up and see me."

As she tried to pull the covers away from her grandma, Mom laughed and smiled. "Well, with that being said, I best get up." Mom tried to get up. She knew she could not do it. The girls crawled in bed with her, though, and that was even better. She is so content when the little ones stop in. They have been her whole life, and now she only can handle it a few minutes. I know this breaks her heart. It is another thing she has had to face.

Darcy, Jade and Megan are here. It is Josh's birthday today. Mom wanted to call him and sing "Happy Birthday." I knew this would be hard for Josh. He was having friends over for pizza/hot tub party, and it was also a going away party for one of their friends who was moving away. He knew that if Grandma were able she would be calling him. She calls him every year to sing to him. He loves it even if she cannot sing. I got home to finish up the party. The kids had a good time. Josh will miss his grandma's way of making his day special.

Friday, January 28, 2005

Dear God, I'm going to be home for some "me time." I will not allow any room for guilt. I have done a good job with Mom, and we still may have a long road yet to go. I just need to keep reminding myself that I have been doing my best.

73

Jeanette said Mom is doing a lot of sleeping today. Jeanette was going to bake some cookies for Mom's company. Mom has a fresh thing in the house for whoever stops by. She loves knowing that when hospice is here, they get coffee and baked items before they go to their next house. She loves lying there and smelling the freshly baked items. She is not really eating anything anymore. I have noticed she has been cutting down on her liquid intake. We could not keep enough Coke in the house before. I had never seen Mom drink a glass of pop until she got cancer.

Darcy and the girls came for the night shift. Darcy helped Mom call me. She calls me when I'm at home. Of course, I do not mind. Darcy was laughing because Mom is always making excuses to call me when I'm not there. I feel so bad about this. It is their time, and she is calling me. I think Mom is using me for a crutch. I work a lot of hours at her house, and she has been leaning on me. I just do not want any hard feelings. We are all loved the same. So much of this is out of my control. We just have to let things fall the way they do. I will accept things for the way they are. We all do our best, and that is all that is expected of us.

Saturday, January 29, 2005

Dear God, there are times this all seems like a bad dream. Help me take a good honest look at what is happening. Keep me strong.

I relieved Darcy this morning. Darcy had been chasing bad guys all night long. Mom has a scanner, and somebody had broken into a café and stolen some money. They had a high-speed chase to catch them. They were driving by the lake, so Darcy saw what was going on. She had to stay awake until they caught them. This went on all night. Mom was mad that she had slept through the whole thing. In the morning, Darcy had to go to work at their meat market. "You cannot stay up all night and chase bad guys and then come to work the next morning," said her husband, Jeremy. We laughed about this. It was a good stress reliever for what we're going through right now.

I was reading my magazine, and when I turned the page, there was a mother and daughter advertisement on cancer. "I'm glad my Mom is here to walk." This hit me like a ton of bricks. I felt like I was hearing

Living for the Moment

this for the first time. I was really facing this cancer. I had a lot of emotions go through me. The thing that I'm grateful for is I have never felt anger at God for letting this happens. Anger is not my friend, and it will not do me any good. I have accepted this plan since day one. I knew I had to if I was going to survive. This ad meant something to me to because Mom is not walking well. We have to hang onto her while we shuffle. We will be using the belt soon to help transport her from the bed. For right now I'm glad she is here to walk just for today. This was a good day for me to look at the truth at what is happening and face this for what it is—the cancer that is controlling our lives.

I got ahold of some package pops. Mom loves popping them or brown paper bags. Her doing that has scared us all. If she can get us, she is happy. She laughed when I showed her what I had brought her. She got a few of them, but then the noise was too much for her. She wants to keep them close for when Chuck and Bruce are here for their shifts. I bet the boys will be impressed.

Sunday, January 30, 2005

Dear God, we are here for another Sunday. I'm so grateful for Sundays. It is a whole day when I can be with Mom. I know that I have become selfish. Everyone has something going on Sundays, so it was easier just to do every Sunday than to have to find someone each Sunday. This is my one and only Mom, so I don't want to be selfish. I'm grateful for all the days and nights we have ahead of us.

Mom slept in this morning. She wanted a big meal, so I cooked up something even though I knew she could not eat. I think she gets the satisfaction of just smelling food cooking. When you get it to her, she cannot eat it or swallow, and sometimes I do not even bring it to her. She does not even remember, unless she makes a comment on the smell.

We had a nap, and then we had some company. Mom does not talk much. She sits and listens now. It was a nice afternoon. She wanted to go in the bedroom early. She is more comfortable in bed. When we were getting her in bed, she ran over my toes with her walker. "Don't you feel bad when you do that?"

She giggled her evil, little giggle. "If I felt bad, I would not keep doing it, and I would not be laughing." We got her in settled into bed,

Brenda Ann Rebelein

and then she had to go to the bathroom. *Okay now,* I thought, *she is testing my patience.* She was saying sorry, but she was laughing. We got her up. I was walking backwards. I know I should have been behind her, but I was not. Her room is so small, and we had the commode there, but she did not want me to have to mess with cleaning it before we go to bed.

I was walking backwards, and she had her walker when we got to the doorway. I was looking down because her doorway was so narrow to go through. She picked her walker up and slammed it up and down really hard. I thought she was falling, so I dove for her to save her fall. She was standing up nice and tall. "What are you doing?" I screamed at her. She laughed so hard, I thought she was going stand there and pee her pants.

"You look like one of the old white horses we used to have on the farm when we used to scare them. The look on your face was priceless." This made her night. She kept laughing every time she looked at me. When she got back in bed, she talked about her childhood living on the farm and the fun they used to have as kids. She had a sheep named Sammy.

She had the radio on low, but she thought it was on too high. This is something different. She usually has her radio and her scanner on so I cannot sleep.

I keep praying for all of us to have strength. Mom is so strong-willed. I feel that is what keeps her going. She was also in perfect health when she got diagnosed with cancer, and it has to take a long time for everything to shut down. This is giving us our time.

She has been sleeping well at night. It is nice having the radio on low.

Monday, January 31, 2005

Dear God, I'm at home for the day. This is my time to catch my breath. I pray for all my blessings in my home and my surroundings. Help guide Jeanette and Mom while they spend their day together.

Jeanette is with Mom today. Once again, Mom insists on cooking. We are at the point where we need to keep her out of the kitchen. She cannot stand for a long time, and she has no strength in her arms. We do not want to have her get hurt. The kitchen is so close, so it is not

Living for the Moment

like we can shut the door and she will forget about it. This is an open area.

She is very weak and confused. I have had to catch her many times already. I try to stay really close to her when she is this weak. I have tried calling there tonight. The phone must be off the hook. Darcy and the girls are here with her, so she is in good hands. Like they say, no news is good news. I will enjoy my evening with my family.

Chapter 5

God, I'm Scared

February 2005

We are facing the sixth month in our cancer journey. I think about what has happened since we brought Mom home from the hospital. It brings a smile to my face. We have had fun and shared good times. We have had bad days, too, but I try not to dwell on them so they will go away and we can enjoy today. Hospice has taught us how to take care of a loved one medically, physically, and emotionally. We have pulled together with a fine group of team players. Things are progressing each month I write in my journal. With my Higher Power by my side, I will not fail.

Tuesday, February 1, 2005

Dear God, I need to stay focused, to keep my strength while I start another day at Mom's. Give me a looking glass so I can see what is best for Mom. Show me the path we should take as You lead the way.

I relieved Darcy this morning. She said they had a good night. Mom went to bed early, and she had a few sips of soup. I'm here for a double shift. When Mom woke up, she had a hard time understanding things. I had to tell and retell her what I wanted her to do. She was confused with something as easy as taking her medication, though it helps having it in pudding or applesauce. We like to change it up for her so she doesn't get sick of the same old thing. The last few days, every time we do something, she thanks us for it. She keeps thanking us over and over. I know she must be scared, even if she has good faith.

She slept from 8:30-1:00. I made her a waffle and some rice pudding. She only had a few bites, but she loved what she had.

When she asks for pain pills, we are supposed to write down the level of pain, but she will not talk about her pain. She just repeats, "I will take a pain pill." She insists on not talking about it, and she will not complain. It amazes us. She tells us there is nothing to complain about. It won't do any good. She has been so positive. If anyone talks negatively, she just has to give the look. Even the grandchildren know the look.

Mom had me pull all the drapes and lock the door. She wanted a no-company day. This is so unusual for her. I called my siblings and told them in case they were planning to stop by. Usually, she lives for her company. She likes to guess who will stop in today. She is always getting surprises. I knew things were changing. It was a feeling I had down inside me. We stayed in her bedroom through the day and night and watched Lifetime movies. She was very quiet. She slept a lot, and she slept through the night.

Wednesday, February 2, 2005

Dear God, help keep Mom safe and comfortable while I go home. Thank You for another day of being together. Our path is changing. It is about acceptance. Guide me each day.

The hospice nurse and bath ladies were there this morning. They noticed the color of her feet is changing and so is her temperature. There have been times when I thought things were changing, but I was wrong. It's not like I have medical experience. I have been a waitress and mowed lawns all my life, so I'm the student here.

Jeanette called me. Mom slept in her chair in the dining room all day. Darcy and the girls spent the night. She had a few sips of soup and went to bed. Jade and Megan help their grandma in bed on the nights they stay there. She is sleeping for hours now. At times, her eyes are half open.

Darcy called me. She was laughing so hard I could hardly understand what she was saying to me. When she laughs that hard, she gets tears in her eyes. I could just picture it. Finally, she told me to watch this one TV show she had on. I knew that if Mom was trying to sleep, she was not going to get any with Darcy laughing so hard. She had me laughing, and I didn't know what I was laughing about. Once she calmed down some, we talked about how we work full-time, do our wife/mom jobs, hurry and pack a bag and get to Mom's. You just get tired. It has to break somewhere. But she had laughter, and what better medicine is there? Besides Darcy's laughter jag, it was an uneventful night.

Thursday, February 3, 2005

Dear God, I can feel each day You have received my prayers. Help us as we see You touching Mom's body. We see the changes before us. Teach me to have love, faith and courage as I look toward the trying days ahead.

Jeanette called me at five in the morning. Her daughter-in-law may be having a miscarriage and is pregnant with twins. I came here to Mom's and worked a double shift. Darcy and Bruce stopped in, and they can see Mom's breathing is changing. One thing we do not do is talk about her health in her bedroom. She told us that she's feeling different. She can't explain it to us, and she can't say it is pain. I gave her a pain pill to help her relax. Mom asked for no company today. I pulled the drapes and locked the doors. I think the visiting is getting too much for Mom. She wants to be up in the dining room with everyone and have something good to eat with coffee. This is not in her plans right now as we see her getting weaker. We are helping her do everything that she could do herself before. Today was a hard day emotionally, but I kept myself busy. I think at times, if Mom did not teach me to be strong, what would have happened to me? She knew she had to toughen me up so I could take care of her. It is not that crying is bad. We have to do it. But right now, we have work to do. I need to stay focused. Her eyes are half open, and her breathing is raspy.

Mom is talking about how this cancer journey is coming to the end. She told me to bring all her pajamas and robes. I explained to her she already had a bath and was nice and clean. She is confused so much of the time. I thought she did not know what she was talking about, but she commanded me to do as I was told. I went and got all these items from her closet.

"Where is your pen and paper? You always have that in your hand. Go get it. You know what I'm talking about." It was right there, so I grabbed something to write with. She told me to hold up a pair of pajamas or a robe, and I attached a name to each article of clothing. When she got done she had to rest a few minutes. "I want you to have

Living for the Moment

a pajama party at your camper, when you are ready, once I have passed and you have had time to heal."

She read off the menu of what I should serve. It was all her favorite things to eat and drinks, including wine coolers. "Do not forget the chocolate and pickles together for dessert. You tell no one about this party, not even Mike. Have a good time and make it a surprise and know that I will be there, too. This is kind of a thank you party from me. I want no tears, just cheers and fun. Put this party on as if I would be doing this myself."

I was speechless. She has given me so many little jobs to do. I will be too busy to grieve. I have things to do for *her*. I laughed at how she would control me even once she was gone. *This will be fun. I will tell no one.* I put all the items back in the closet while I got my thoughts together. Mom always seems to surprise us.

She called me in her bedroom. She wanted to be reassured that her funeral was ready. We went over it all again like we had done so many times. One night we even acted it out. If someone would have stopped in, they would of sent us both away. We had to laugh at ourselves. We were having her funeral with the music and the reading of the poems. "Sorry, Mom, I do not know the sermon."

I was sitting in a chair, reading the poem I had written and planned to read at the funeral. "Are you going to be sitting while reading this?" she asked me.

"Well no, for dumb."

She laughed, "This is serious. We are practicing. I want to see what my funeral will be like. This is going to be nice. I wish I could sit there, too. Maybe I will come to see how you all do." This woman is something else. How many people act out their own funeral? Tonight she was satisfied that everything was settled for her final send off.

She would be talking to me, and then she would slip away for a few seconds. Then she would come back to the conversation. She wouldn't remember what she was talking about. I would act like I forgot, too, so she would not feel bad. It bothers her when her mind slips. She slept the rest of the day and night. I hate the thought of leaving her tomorrow. Each day the doors are closing in on us.

Friday, February 4, 2005

Dear God, it is so hard to leave Mom this morning. I'm going to stay one more day. It worked out in my favor because we needed someone for today. I was selfish and agreed to stay. I know this may be dumb God, but right now I can reach out and touch her. There will be a day when I cannot do this, when she goes to a better place. I know You are getting her place ready, and she will be called home soon.

Mom was better today. She was happy about leaving her bedroom for a few minutes.

Jade and Megan went to see her after school and stayed until Darcy could come and get them. Mom smiles when her grandchildren come and see her. Megan wanted to play beauty shop. She got all set up for her new business. She did our hair and our nails. The name of her shop was Megan's Glamour Salon. It made us all giggle doing "girl" things. Mom enjoyed herself. Once her nails were dry, I put her diamond ring back on her finger. I like seeing it on her, and she likes it on my finger. I wish she would wear it until she takes her last breath, but she has lost so much weight that she is afraid she will lose it. I'm so happy when we get these final good memories that will last a lifetime. We are lucky to get this chance. I will be passing Mom's ring down to Jade. It will keep going down through the generations of girls.

Late in the afternoon, I said to Mom, "Let's get out of this bedroom. You have been in here for a few days. I will help you into the wheelchair, and you can sleep in your chair if you get tired." It was a nice afternoon out in the dining room, watching people walking around the lake. When I was putting her to bed, Thelma stopped in with groceries. Soon, here came Sheila, Monica, Paul, and then, last but not least, Chuck. They all went and sat in Mom's little bedroom in chairs, on the floor, or they crawled into bed with her. The little bedroom, as Mom always called it, was full. They got their favorite beverage and talked about the past times we had together. They were teasing each other and laughing. Mom would fall asleep for a few minutes, but she did not want anyone to leave. "If you get boring, I will sleep until I wake up." Mom would point her index finger at somebody and give him or her some advice they should listen to. "Charlie, you better watch out for the yellow butterfly." We all laughed. She told Thelma, "You know you are driving my son's car." She fell asleep then, and they left, but she did not notice until a long time later. It was a night we will always remember.

I slept in the chair next to her bed. Her breathing has changed so much. "Sentimental Journey" came on the radio three times during the night. The second time it came on, Mom was moaning really loudly. It scared me as we only have on a small night-light. She made loud noises all night long. It was hard to tell if she was in pain. At times she was reaching up in the air and moaning. It looked like she was trying to get to someone. Was she talking to an angel? Is my Dad calling her? As I watched, this fear became a comfort, knowing she was going home soon. She would be in a place where there is no pain. You go to be with your loved ones that are waiting for you. This gave me a peaceful feeling. She reached into the air and moaned for someone through the night.

Saturday, February 5, 2005

Dear God, the last two days were hard on me. Later this will be a warm feeling when I remember this moment. We can really see Mom slipping. How many times have we said that? These are the stages we have to go through. Being a witness last night to Mom reaching out is something so worthwhile to watch. It was so peaceful. I just wanted to help her go in peace. To be part of this journey has been an honor. Thank You, God, for the memories.

Today I came home. Chuck is going to do a double shift at Mom's. I made her a waffle and hot tea before I left. I talked to Chuck late in the day. She had slept all day long, but she did get up at suppertime. One time awhile back, she told Darcy and me, when she got her cancer news, that she would not be a complainer, no matter how tough things get. This is one promise she has kept. She has been so easy to take care of. Yes, we have had our bad days, but you forget about them. They were not in our control. It is good being back at home, but my heart is at Mom's.

Sunday, February 6, 2005

Dear God, guide Mom through the day. Please bring us through safely while we go snow tubing for Megan's tenth birthday. Jeremy, Darcy, Jade and Megan have invited

Brenda Ann Rebelein

Mike, Josh and me to go along with ten classmates of Megan's. Hear me pray. I do not like heights, speed, and snow. Hear my prayer.

Darcy feels I need a break at Mom's. She will not take no for an answer, so I will be going snow tubing. I know it will be good for me. Chuck said he would stay the day until I got back.

It was a fun and scary day. Megan's classmate's wanted to go down the hill with Darcy. We had a blast. It was good medicine for me.

I called Mom to tell her how the day was going. She wanted me to call and tell her about all the fun the kids were having. Her voice was so weak. She wished us a good time and to be careful that we did not break anything. When I got off the phone, Darcy told me that I needed to start preparing myself for her death. I will not be able to run to the phone to call her anymore. I know she is right.

Then we were off to Godfather's Pizza for pizza and cake and gift opening for the birthday girl. She got a lot of nice gifts.

While we were eating, it started snowing pretty well. I called Jeanette to see if she could go to Mom's to stay. She said she would. I will have to do snow removal with Mike. Mom was quiet and rested all day for Chuck. Bruce went and got more medication for her. They have added more medication to keep her comfortable. When we got home, it really hit me that we will be losing her. I thought about how many times I call her for something or just to talk about nothing really. It was a lonely feeling.

It is hard to get to sleep. That is one thing I have learned in the hospice books. It is normal that it is hard for us to sleep at night when losing a loved one. I sit up all hours of the night. I'm getting scared and happy for her all at the same time. I want to be there so bad when she starts her new life. I'm so afraid I will not be there. I do not know God's plans for me. If it is meant to be, I will be there. It may come to the time when Mom does not want anyone close to her when she leaves to go with God. My faith has been strong.

She had slept all day. Jeanette had to wake her to take her medications at 8 p.m. Today I tried to think about my life without her. Right now I'm so busy taking care of her. There will be that void in my life. The main thing is that she will be fine and so will I. She has taught me how to survive.

84

Living for the Moment

She is not herself anymore. In her mind, she has somewhat already moved on. The whole family life has revolved around our mom and grandma.

Mike and Josh have been so good to me, letting me spend all the hours that I do at my Mom's. When I have to go extra hours, they just said, "Go, We will be fine. We will do what you have to do." I tease them that it looks better when I'm not here. The hours that I miss out in our business, he hires out, and he makes medication runs when needed. They bring us supper over to Mom's, so there is no cooking in the house. They come over to see Mom. He lets me vent when I need it or when he has to pull it out of me to make me feel better. There are not enough words to express my gratitude to my husband. I need to remember she is still my patient. She will be Mom soon, in God's time.

Monday, February 7, 2005

Dear God, You know my emotions are running wild here. Mom is up and all excited. The last time I was there she was down in bed and not getting out. Now they cannot keep her in bed. Please God, help me slow down and get control over myself. Hear my prayer.

Jeanette is still with Mom. She said Mom was up every hour on the hour all night. I called hospice to see what they think is going on with her. Is she having pain and cannot tell us? Is that is why she is antsy? They say a patient will have a surge of energy, and she has had many. She has gone over the books. The nurse is scheduled to be there in the morning. We will give her extra anxiety medications and see if that helps. I asked them a lot of questions. We have never done this before. They told me Mom would not fail until she is in bed all the time and does not get up at all. Then there will be no more eating, no more drinking, and apnea. We are getting so tired. Hospice is so wonderful to help us out with everything. We would not be at home without hospice. It's more than just helping us with her baths and medication. They will be our friends forever.

Darcy, Jade and Megan are at Mom's for the night shift. I hope everything goes well for them and that Mom will rest.

Brenda Ann Rebelein

Tuesday, February 8, 2005

Dear God, I'm at Mom's now for the day shift. It is good coming home. Each day I think of the blessings I have, and it does not take that long to have a nice list. That is what we need to keep reminding ourselves. I feel we are counting the days now. Too much is happening. I'm so glad we have had the opportunity to keep Mom at home. I pray this wish will continue to come true until the end.

I relieved Darcy this morning. It was a bad night for them. It was about three in the morning when Mom did a lot of vomiting. They were trying to clean her up. She did not understand what they were saying to her; she was very confused. When they would get her cleaned up, she would vomit again. Then she was at the end of the bed, holding on to it. She would not move or let go of the bed. She had a tight grip on it. Her legs were stiff as boards and she could not bend them. This went on a long time. Finally, they got her back in bed. She started screaming. Darcy should have called for help. She said there was so much going on, and they did not have time to call anyone. I'm sure they were glad to leave this morning. This is the first bad night when the girls were there. We will see how things go. It is up to Darcy and Jeremy when they think the girls should not come anymore. The girls have learned about death firsthand. They have been taking care of their dying grandma. Jeremy has to work, and they are too young to be left alone. We need Darcy here. They go down in the living room and spend their time when grandma is bad. I feel bad for all of them today.

The nurse was here, and she is going to give Mom more pain medication. She gave her a very good checkup this morning, and she will call me later this afternoon. We cannot talk in front of Mom. She is very confused and does not understand what we are saying. She went right to sleep.

Little Blake, who lives next door, asked, "Mommy, is Grandma Marvel going to die?"

"Yes, honey, she is."

He thought for a moment. "How do I get her to heaven?"

Sheila was surprised this was coming out of her four-year-old's mouth. Sheila explained to him that God will call her name, and she will follow Him, then He will get her to heaven. "Where did you learn this Blake?" she asked him.

Living for the Moment

He looked at his Mom long and hard. "My brain just tells me it." We decided maybe it is time to call the nieces to see if they want their kids to talk to a social worker. We do not want any confused kids. It is time we have the help for them if needed. They came after school and met at Sheila's. The social worker thinks the kids are doing great. We have involved them in everything that has happened. I think that has helped.

Mom and I talked between her naps. "Mom, what do you think dad would say if you showed up in heaven for Valentines Day?" She turned to me and just smiled. Then she looked away from me. "Call Pastor Soli. I want communion."

She would not look at me. I felt bad, like maybe I should not have said that. Pastor Soli came, and Mom had communion. I gave her this time with Pastor Soli alone. We've had our time as a family. She needs her privacy as she prepares to go to heaven. Pastor Soli and Pastor Gary have been so good to us.

Mom has been in bed all day. She has not moved. I have kept it quiet here today. Mike called me, and more snow is on the way. I called Bruce and he will come take over for me so I can go home and work. We have a lot of businesses we take care of with snow removal, so we need to be ready when needed. Jeanette came in for the night shift. They had a quiet night. I'm sure Jeanette was ready for a quiet night.

Wednesday, February 9, 2005

Dear God, yesterday is in the past. Let me enjoy this day You have given me. Our snowfall was a blessing. It separated me from the cancer situation for a little while. I tried to do meditation to clear my mind.

I worked hard with this snowfall. We kept getting more calls than usual. That is what we want to keep the business going. I had to get to Mom's to do the night shift. Jeanette was there for the day shift. Mom had a bath this morning. They changed her medication again. It is good that we have them out in containers for each dose we have to give her. Darcy is our main pill person. The new changes they make in Mom's medication always seem to work. They know what they are doing. They never ask questions; they just make it better. We noticed her legs are getting harder. They are like stiff boards. Darcy found that

Brenda Ann Rebelein

out when she had Mom by the bed. Mom could not move. This, I'm sure, is another sign that things are progressing. Her face is turning jaundiced. It runs from her forehead to her nose, mouth and chin. She does not look in the mirror much anymore. I know this would bother her if she saw it. One day she looked in the mirror and was shocked at how old she looked. I tried to sugar coat it and tell her that I think she looks the same.

It is hard having any conversation with her. It is like she is in a fog and looking right through me. She will spring a joke on us, though, once in awhile. Then she'll turn her head and smile. It is nice to see the old Mom coming out. She got her hair done. It took a lot out of her to get this done. She could not get back in bed fast enough. She doesn't order tons of hair spray anymore or hair color. I remember the day she was antsy and I had to hide all the air fresheners and hairsprays under her bed. We are always teasing her about her coloring her hair. It is coal black. She slept the rest of the day.

Before she got sick, reading was a big part of Mom's life. She keeps trying to read. She was reading a paragraph before she fell asleep. Now she just sleeps with the book in her hand. Tonight Mom wanted to get up and make some supper. I knew that was impossible for her. I had to give her some medication to keep her down. That was a big step for me when we first started taking care of her. I did not want to be responsible for keeping her down in bed. I have learned it is not about me. What the patient needs is more important. She is not even eating anything anymore except waffles filled with lots of syrup and butter. She just wants to cook, but she is at the stage where she can hurt herself or others.

We are getting so tired and drained. This could get to be too much for our shoulders. We need to know that we all did our best. We feel like walking zombies. We keep going and try not to think about it. Will we get to fulfill Mom's wish of staying in her own home? It soon could be out of our hands, and they will have to take her to a hospice room in the hospital or put her in the rest home. Please, God, don't let this happen. We need to feel our guardian angel near us.

Mom slept all night.

Thursday, February 10, 2005

Dear God, I love my home, and I am home for the day. I want some kind of relief from this situation we are all living. Mom has had so many bursts of energy. We have been saying that at times she is doing better than us. We are drained, emotionally and physically. This is something we need to do and want to do. This is a wonderful way to repay her for what she has done for us through the years. Give us a peaceful rest. Sometimes your body just says enough is enough. I cannot sleep at night. I will face whatever we are given now that we are making another turn.

Darcy is at home and Jeanette is with Mom. Darcy reached her breaking point. She had a good cry. I was so jealous of her. She feels so much better. I have tried to really break myself and nothing happens. My strong feelings get in the way. Mom is happy where she is at and where she is going. We have had many years of good memories, and we are still building. There is nothing to be sad about. I wonder is my wall built up that high? Have I just accepted that this is Mom's time? I feel I can take care of me later. I know myself as Mom knows me. If I fall, I will fall hard. I'm so afraid I will not get a hold of myself. I spend too many hours at Mom's. She needs me. I need to be strong. I need her to be my patient. When my work is done, she can be Mom again. I need to stay focused. After I talked to Darcy, I thought about this. Maybe I should force myself to cry. I got an old Christmas video tape out. Mom was laughing and hugging all the kids and she was hollering at the adults in a good way. She does not like cameras or being taped. Mike was walking room to room taping everyone. Mom yelled at him to bring the camcorder into the kitchen. She had him walk with her as she introduced him to our Christmas dinner that she made all herself: goose, duck, and ham for meat, mashed potatoes and gravy; corn; dressing with raisins; two relish trays and salads. We all brought the desserts. Her favorite was pecan pie or fudge or any chocolate with pickles. She showed him the items for oyster stew. Then she shooed him out of her kitchen. When I got done watching the tape I could not cry. I had my Kleenex ready. It made me smile. What an amazing woman we have had in our life. She teases me now that things are progressing. If she is counting on us, she could be in trouble. She cannot believe how we have all pulled together and made this happen since the day she came home from the hospital. She talks about how grateful she is. Bruce is here during the day, Chuck is here at night.

She had a bath today. They gave her a sponge bath in bed. It is impossible for her to use the bathtub. She is wild and wants to get out of bed. We know it is not possible for her to do the things she used to, but it is hard to get this through to her. If we could get her into the wheelchair so she could be in the dining room and look out her deck window, she would be happy. She gets near that kitchen and she is ready to cook a feast. "What's on the menu? What are you hungry for?" She does not understand that she has cooked her last meal. This went on the whole day with her wanting to get up. She was wild and excited. Jeanette had to give her the maximum dose of anxiety medication. If she would go to the dining room and sit, she would be okay, but she wants to get up and walk or go to the kitchen. She will not stay put. We have made it this far without her falling. Hospice is walking Jeanette through the day.

When Darcy, Jade and Megan got there for the night shift, Mom was reading the paper in bed. Then she tried to get up and walk away from her bed. She has no strength to stand up or pull herself up on her own. Darcy got her to go to the bathroom; we are using the commode next to the bed. The bathroom is too far for Mom to walk. The nurse has been telling Mom this. They tell her, "You are all wore out by the time you get to the bathroom, and then you have to walk back. You need to save your energy." She just does not understand this. They got her on the commode okay. When it came time to get her back in bed, she fell face down in bed. It just proved to her that she cannot walk. She knew then that the nurse was right; she could not walk anymore. Darcy handled it well.

Friday, February 11, 2005

Dear God, Mom is doing somewhat better today. I'm slowing things down once again for me. I have a way I bolster my emotions when I know there is a change, and I know when I need to slow things down for me. Lately, I have not been living for the moment. I keep thinking of the future and that is getting me in trouble. I need to live for now. Baby steps are my new plan to survive.

Living for the Moment

Jeanette is with Mom today. Her new medications are working; she is comfortable in bed. I feel so bad when Jeanette has a bad day at Mom's. I know there is nothing she would not do for Mom. They have been friends for many years. It started when Jeanette married my dad's nephew. Jeanette and Mom have formed a strong relationship through the years. "This is a way I can repay her for all the years she helped me out," Jeanette said.

Mom is not trying to get out of bed today. That is a blessing. Sometimes you wonder where all her strength is coming from. Bruce stayed with Mom in the afternoon. Chuck had the night shift. She slept all day. Tonight at 8:30, Chuck helped Mom call me. She told Chuck she had to talk to me. When I got on the phone, there was nothing on the other end of the line, but then I heard, "I want to talk to you. The end is near for me, so you need to prepare yourself. What is the schedule and who has the next few days?" I had to listen really closely. She was soft spoken.

"Chuck is there tomorrow. Darcy will be there tomorrow night. Bruce and I are a call away. I will be there Sunday like always." She was quiet for a few minutes. "I do not know if I will make it that long. Chuck will call you if I pass away. I know the end is near. Please stay close to your phone." I was so speechless. This was not a call I was thinking about getting. She thanked me for getting her comfortable again with the medications. I had nothing to do with it. We talked about her wild day in bed. She remembers only parts of it. She felt bad for Jeanette. She asked me if I thought if it was okay if she stayed in bed all the time now. I told her I thought it was the best thing for her. She feels no pain. We did not talk much more after that. She was getting weaker and more tired the longer we talked. I'm at the point where I enjoy any conversation I have with Mom now. We do not talk much anymore. She sleeps a lot. Chuck called later—the night went well.

Saturday, February 12, 2005

Dear God, I'm having a sad day today. I have not had one in a long time. I'm feeling my loss. I'm trying to be strong like Mom has taught me. Does she know how much each member of the family loves her? Please give her my message. I do not know what she understands anymore. I hope we can get her comfortable so she will stay safe in bed

91

Brenda Ann Rebelein

while we circle around her. I'm so grateful for hospice, family and friends. Without teamwork, this would be impossible. God bless everyone.

Chuck had a quiet night with Mom. She slept all day. She told Chuck she was not far from dying and asked if he would stay close by. Darcy had the night shift. She helped Mom call me tonight. She wanted to talk to me again. She said she missed me. I wanted to make light of the conversation, so I told her she tells that to everyone that stays with her. She told me she would be dying soon. She would try to wait until my shift tomorrow morning. She was so weak and soft spoken; I had to really listen to her. We tried to laugh about dumb things we have done. Humor has been a big part of this process, to keep it light. Laughter is the best medicine no matter what situation we are in. Mom will have humor all the way to her grave. Darcy has been reading the Bible to Mom. She is finding comfort in this. I'm glad Mom can pray again. We all need that right now.

Sunday, February 13, 2005

Dear God, You have answered my prayers. Mom is staying in bed and resting comfortably. Guide us each day and night while we take care of our loved one, Marvel Mae.

Darcy and Mom put in a long night last night. Mom dreamed that people were pulling her out of bed, and she was trying to get out of bed to go with them. People were talking to her. She did a lot of screaming. I feel it was the angels coming to prepare Mom for her journey. This went on through the night, and Darcy was so tired when I got there. She had to go to work for the day. When you are up all night and then have to put in a full day's worth of work, it makes it hard. They just opened up their meat market business. The first year is the tough one.

I will be here for a double shift. Mom is having a lot of hot flashes, so that is making her very restless. She is doing a lot of screaming during her sleep. We've seen this at night, but this is the first time I have seen it during the day. I'm sitting next to her bed, rubbing her arms and talking softly so she knows someone is near her. When Mom was growing up, her sister used to touch her shoulders at bedtime. That drove Mom nuts. Her mom would make her sister sleep that way. When

92

Living for the Moment

she grew up, she hated when someone would touch her shoulders. She would yell if we did it. Now on this cancer journey, she does not mind it. One time when we stayed at a casino, I waited until she was in a very sound sleep. We were sleeping in the same bed, so I touched her shoulders to see if it really would bother her. She jumped in bed and yelled. Mike, Josh and I laughed so hard.

Mom woke up from a rest and wanted to call a few people to say goodbye and thank them for what they had done for her since she's been home. This call had to be hard for them to receive. When Mom was on a mission, nothing stopped her. She always got that extra energy. Mom has been restless today as she sleeps. She kept moaning over and over, "Ten thousand dollars." I got up from the chair and leaned close to her to hear what she was saying. A few minutes later, as I was starting to sit back down, I heard Mom whisper, "Write a book." I was shocked. It was like I was not hearing right. Was she coaching me to write about our cancer journey? We had talked about it when she first got home, when she caught me writing about her. I have also shown her all the poems I wrote during this journey. I started this journal to help me with my feelings. Everyone has a way of dealing with his or her emotions. My escape is in writing. I think if I had not been standing there, I would not have heard her. Did she know I was there? I will never know. *God bless you, Mom.*

Mom woke up at suppertime and had to use the commode. She can only go three steps, so we have the commode right there. She is dead weight. We are using the transfer belt to move her, and we have to roll her in bed. She has no strength to move herself. We have been rolling her every three hours so she can get her legs and back rubbed since she is spending so much time in her bed now. I will not let her get bedsores.

Darcy and I were talking, and we may team up together and "two man" our shifts. It is getting to be too much for one person. With Mom sleeping so much it would be nice to have the company. We were laughing at how we can hardly get the schedule filled with one person, and now we need two per shift. This could get interesting. Who knows if this is her last week with us? We need to be prepared. We are all in God's hands. He has answered so many of my prayers. I feel I have a direct line to Him.

Brenda Ann Rebelein

When we were driving over here, it was quiet in the pickup. Mike and I were lost in our own thoughts. Then he said to me, "We know your mom does not have much time left. You spend a lot of hours over here. When you are at home or working with me, you are still thinking of your mom, and that is normal. I feel you are only happy when you are with your mom; so if you want to stay with her until she passes away, it is okay with Lance, Josh and me. We can do the business. We have been doing it so much now anyway. What are a few more hours a day? I can bring you clothes as you need them."

I could not say anything with the tears starting to fall from my cheeks. What a gift he has given me. I have never loved him more than that moment, when he did such an unselfish act. "Thank you, I would like that. I will make this up to you when this is over." I could not wait to get out of the pickup to tell Mom the news, even if she was not talking. The tears fell down her cheeks when I told her she was stuck with me until the end. She never said a word. I guess she did not have to.

Mom had me call the hospice office. She just wanted them on the phone. By the time the phone was ringing, she was sleeping. I woke her when I got the nurse on the line. She wanted to thank them for all their hard work, and the care they had given her. She was failing, and her time was coming soon. She wished them a good life and lots of happiness.

She is still wearing her oxygen, yet she is still having a hard time with breathing. I reassured her again that I was told she would have a peaceful death. She wants me to keep reminding her of this. Mom was talking about some unfinished business. I had heard that from the books we got from hospice. A loved one who is dying needs to take care of all their business before they can pass away. Sometimes they hang on until it is taken care of. They call it unfinished business. There is one thing Mom has that is unfinished but will never be taken care of. She will have to pass away without it completed. We have talked about it. She has to accept it for what it is—unfinished business.

There was another part of her unfinished business that we could make happen. She had a gift she wanted to give to someone. I told Mom that I had the gift here, and it was in the kitchen. There was a look of shock on her face, and she thought I was lying. She looked at me in

Living for the Moment

disbelief, so I went and got it. She cried so hard. We have never been a hugging family, but we all knew the love was there. She hugged me so tight, and she was so overjoyed. She had me call her favorite person to come see her and receive the gift. She kept crying and hugging me. "Thank you, thank you! You are an angel. I love you, I love you." It tore my heart apart to think we almost did not get this task completed. This was one more wish that did come true. I gave them some alone time. It will be a moment they will always remember. Lance came and spent the rest of the day with us. He went and got us something to eat. Mom was sleeping.

Vicki came with her kids. They live an hour away from Mom. They do not get to see her as much as we do. Vicki comes when she can. Mom loves when she gets to see her and her family. They knew this was the last time they were going to get to see Grandma. They all took their turns going in there, seeing her. She would not allow tears. She told them each how much they meant to her and what she expects them to do with their lives. "Always be happy and make the best out of your lives." It was hard for them to go home. They knew this was so final. Mom was proud of how strong everyone was. It helps her. If everyone cries, what a mess that would be. How many times has Mom told me that?

It was the end of the day. I was getting ready for bed. Mom was sleeping on and off. Mary Lou, stopped and helped me get Mom on the commode and back in bed. Mary Lou is in town staying with her son. This proved we need two people. I could never do it alone. She really is dead weight, and I'm not experienced in this field. She is stuck with what hospice is teaching me. Bruce is stopping a lot during the day, and that helps when you need an extra hand. We have created a care-giving support team. Emotionally we do not have to walk alone. I have called a few people to tell them that I will be staying until the end. This is what I need for me. I want be with Mom when she crosses the finish line of this cancer journey. When I'm at home, I pray, *Please do not let her die today.*

Monday, February 14, 2005

Dear God, I see Mom is slowly giving up her control. We have laughed and teased her for planning when and how and what she was going to do when she got to heaven.

95

It is time, while she rests so peacefully, to give up the control. I helped her pray this prayer. "I pray to you, God, each day. It is time to give up the control and step aside, until You call my name. I will see my loved ones soon. Then my cancer journey will come to an end, in God I pray."

Mom had a peaceful night. Her breathing was shallow, and her body made quick jerks, but there was no screaming like the night before. She told me that she feels safe when we are all here. She wishes we could all just stay here until she passes away. The reality is that they have to work. We have had a good connection during this journey. This is better than I could have ever dreamed. Then for Mike to come up with letting me stay … words cannot express what this means to me.

Mary Lou came to stay with Mom. I went for an hour-long walk around the lake. It was great getting some fresh air and getting away from the situation for a few minutes.

Darcy came and stayed the night with Mom and me. Monday nights are her night to stay. We had fun watching TV in Mom's bedroom, just us three girls. Mom showed us some humor tonight. She was too weak to get up, so she wanted us to try using the bedpan for the first time. We had lots of giggles. She knows we are not nurse material. We were laughing. None of us knew what we were doing. We did pretty well once we got the hang of it. Mom loved having Darcy and me together like this. We should have done this sooner.

Courtney stopped to see mom, she was sleeping. She sat next to mom's bed for an hour. When mom woke up. She asked me. "What did Courtney want?' I replied "Nothing. She was quiet for a minute."I thought she wanted something, and was afraid to ask. What teenager just sits next to a grandma's for so long." I told her to remember how much they all love you.

The grandchildren stopped in and had Valentine treats to show Grandma. They danced enough to make her smile. The little ones only stay a little while. It is hard for Mom to send them away, but any noise is hard on her. Mom's girlfriend from Arizona is coming late Wednesday night. They both cannot wait to see each other. We had a laid back night. Mom received flowers from a girlfriend. I received some from Mike.

Sisters are for secrets. Darcy and I had one to share. We did some laughing tonight, knowing we would not tell. I thought for sure that Mom would give us a holler to quiet us down. We tried to get some sleep, but the giggles kept coming. This is what sisters are for—the secrets you do not have to share and the laughter which is good medicine.

Wednesday, February 15, 2005

Dear God, I thank You for the hospice care and the wonderful medication we can give Mom to keep her comfortable. I pray each day she will go peacefully. You keep her here one more day. I feel You with me each day with the power of prayer. I will spend the days with Mom. I embrace what you give me.

Mom woke up in a good mood. She was rested and was holding a good conversation. She laughed at what we had giggled about last night. "I heard you giggling; it was like you were little kids again." She enjoyed lying there, listening to us. We did not know she was awake. She wanted to know who could sleep with the way we were laughing.

Mom visited for about an hour, and then she had a quick catnap. Sometimes she just closes her eyes and listens to what everyone else has to say. I brought her company into the bedroom. They did not stay long because she kept falling asleep. She looks so comfortable in bed. I, too, fell asleep in the chair next to her bed. When I woke up, we had company. They were just waiting for us to wake up. Mom teased them and wanted to know if lunch was ready. She only eats waffles, pudding, and applesauce. They had a nice visit.

Later, Mom had a room full of grandchildren: Bruce, Spenser, Tessa, Nathanial, Aurora, Jeremy, and Mayson who are Bruce and Wendy's family. I gave them their time alone. Mayson sat on the bed with Mom and had crackers and cookies. She wanted to make a mess so I could clean it up. Darcy came, and we went for a walk. The grandchildren stayed with Mom while we were gone. It is good to have fresh air and not have to think of the bedpan and medication. Today the death rattle started. I can smell death in her room. We had someone get some air fresheners to put around the room. It was early when Mom went to sleep for the night. She had a lot of company today.

Brenda Ann Rebelein

Wednesday, February 16, 2005

Dear God, I'm on my fourth day of being at Mom's. Each day that I stay, we are blessed with another one. I have slowed things down for me, as you know. I have been doing one hour at a time. There is so much to do here each day. I know we are getting closer to the end. I'm glad everyone stops and says hi, even if we have to wake her up.

Mom has been sleeping well at night. It helps us all. Bruce has been staying close and that has helped. He is not doing bed pan duty yet. Little does he know his time is coming. We are not using the commode, except for bowel movements. It is too hard for Mom to get in and out of bed, so we use the bedpan. Sometimes it is good, and then others, we do not talk about it. We just get more bedding. When I'm here alone, I know it will be bad for Mom and me to do the commode alone. "What is easiest for you?" she asked. I wanted to say *neither one*. I knew I could not do that. She is still thinking of others. We agreed the bedpan is the best. She does not want to be a burden to us. As we learn, Mom laughs or prays to God to help her. She thinks we are idiots. We tease her, saying we will be pro's when we learn our job.

Mom and I overflowed the bedpan. We were laughing so hard. It was a mess. "You should have showed me to do bedpans once in awhile rather than serving hamburgers," I told her.

"You worked in a rest home once, when I fired you that time."

"Funny, Mom. Haha." I told her she would now have limits to her beverages. It's good that it's bath day for her. I got a lesson from the nurse and bath lady in bedpan use.

Mom slept a lot today. She wants her rest. She knows her friend is coming, and she does not want to be tired when she gets here. Darcy came and spent the night with us. It is fun having just the girls. You are never too old for a slumber party. This journey has brought us all closer together.

Jeremy, Jade, and Megan came to have supper with Darcy. They stayed for awhile, then they went home. It is hard for the kids to understand all this. We are here so much of the time. It has been hard on our home lives. They know we are doing it because we love Grandma. When all the grandchildren crawl in bed with Mom, it breaks my heart. But it also it gives me a warm fuzzy feeling to know that they are getting these special moments. We had a nice night with Mom, but by the end of the night, she was too weak to respond. It is hard to understand how quickly things change around here.

Thursday, February 17, 2005

Dear God, I'm so glad You kept Mom alive so she can see her friend one more time. They now can have their final time together. Thank you for another peaceful night.

When Karen got here in the middle of the night, she wanted to peek in at Mom just to look at her. She crawled right in bed with her, and they held each other so tight. We got some sleep. Then in the morning, she woke Mom up. You could tell by the look on Mom's face, she did not recognize her. After a few minutes, Mom put this big smile on her face. "You made it. I was hoping I would get to see you one more time." They had a good time. I made them breakfast and served it in Mom's bedroom, but I do not want them to get used to this service. You know what was on the menu? Nothing but waffles and hot tea. They spent the morning in Mom's bedroom. They had a lot of catching up to do. Mom was talking and understanding the conversations, though once in awhile she would get lost. I gave them their time alone.

Karen went to visit her mom and sister for the day. That would give Mom time to rest. She slept all day today. When Karen got back, they talked about old times and how Mom was getting herself ready to go to heaven. Mom told us that she sees dad more and more all the time. He looks so handsome, and sometimes he is in his uniform from the service. He wants her to come with him. "Why don't you follow him?" I asked her.

"I could not get out of bed," she replied. She still cannot get out of bed alone. She has been in the bedroom a long time. It is easier when she does not want to leave. It is safer for all of us.

These two gals were meant to be together one more time.

Mom is hearing noises in the middle of the night. You know it's angels coming to see her. She wants me to keep sleeping in the chair next to her bed. No one else can do that. I can sleep anywhere, and she is afraid to be alone at night. I can see she is having pain, but she still will not complain. We still listen to her funeral music. Karen is staying with us. She will be leaving to go see her daughter and her family. It is

Brenda Ann Rebelein

nice having her here. I will miss waking up and not seeing Mom's face lying next to me. For now, this is our moment to embrace.

Friday, February 18, 2005

Dear God, I'm going to go home for two days. Mom has caught another burst of conversation. She still stays in her bedroom. With her friend here, it is time for me to go home and get refreshed for when she leaves. Guide my mom. Keep a hand on my shoulders while You keep me strong. Watch over my patient, Marvel Mae. Please guide the caretakers and hospice staff as they do their job each day.

It was hard for me to leave her. She asked me not to go. I knew I needed to take care of myself so I could take care of her. Darcy will be here for the day. She is in good hands. It is time for them to have their time alone, too. Karen went to see family, and she will be back tonight. It is so nice having her here. Mom is still sleeping off and on. She has been talking with her eyes closed. She is still getting a bath three days a week. The hospice nurses comes every other Tuesday until something more changes. They said her blood pressure is down and her pulse is slower since the last time they were here. It can only be weeks now. Only God knows. If she is seeing Dad, it might not be much longer.

It is nice having the comforts of my own home. I'm so lucky to have a family that allows me to be with my dying mother. Chuck has the night shift at Mom's. They called me, and they were laughing and having a good time in her little bedroom. Karen came back from visiting. She is going to go for a few days to be with her daughter and family. If Mom were to die tonight, she would die so happy. It was like old times. They always had a good time together with lots of laughs. God will have to make room for a cheerful, happy person who loves a good time—our mom, grandma, and friend.

Saturday, February 19, 2005

Dear God, we all need Your strength to carry us through each hour. Chuck called me at 4:30 am. I need to go help him with Mom. Things are changing again. She is vomiting up blood. I will receive with open arms what You have planned for her.

Mike drove me to Mom's right after we got the call from Chuck. When we got there, Chuck told us Mom had been vomiting blood since

Living for the Moment

3:00 am. I helped him get her cleaned up. By the time we had gotten there, he had her cleaned her up once and put a new gown on her, but it didn't do any good. It was like old coffee grounds.

I told Mom that I had talked to Dad. He wants her to come to heaven to be with him. I reassured her that everyone in the family would be okay. Hospice taught us, when it comes to the end, we need to show our loved ones that we will all be okay when they are gone. She was resting well once we got her cleaned up again and put new bedding on the bed. She had lost control of her urine. It is easy now to change her bedding with her still in bed. We have gotten good at this rolling business. Chuck went to lie down. I think he was sleeping before he hit the pillow.

It is time now to run our shifts with two people. During the day it is not so bad because there is always someone around to help. I knew this was necessary last Sunday when Mom called some people and said good-bye and thanked them for being her friend and helping her. She told them to always stay happy. I thought then that Mom knew something. I have heard that a person knows when they are dying. When Mom has had company, she has told everyone it will not be much longer. "Do not cry. I have had a good life. It is time to move on. I'm excited about my new beginning, and you should be happy for me." We all have heard this speech. This is a remarkable woman.

She has seen Dad twice. The person she wants to see the most is her grandma. I was glad I had asked her that before she got so sick.

Karen and Mom have had a good time. They visit, and then Mom will rest once in awhile. This has been a long week for us.

When Chuck woke up, Mom called for him to help her into her wheelchair. She had this unknown strength. She was not taking no for an answer, and she wanted to go into the dining room. We tried talking her out of it. Finally, he knew it was best to do as she said. *What is she up to now?* Chuck rolled her out to the dining room, and she insisted on getting to the deck window. She kept falling asleep, and we watched her, silently, shaking our heads. Once in awhile she would look out the window, and then her head would drop down. This went on for an hour. "I wanted to see the geese on the lake one more time. I love looking out this window from my nice deck. I will always remember this moment," she said. "I'm ready to go back to bed. Will you help me Chuck?" This took a lot out of her; she was so weak again. This unknown strength is something we will never understand.

Mom's hands are starting to look crippled up, her eyes are half-open and her breathing is so shallow. Chuck is staying the night with me. I think he likes me. I have told him this is our bonding time. For supper, we had tomato soup, American fries, and macaroni and cheese. They were leftovers from when we brought food. We do not cook for her because we do not want Mom to smell food or see us eat. We laughed about this, though, since Mom would not be impressed with our cooking skills tonight.

Pastor Gary was here today. Mom did not respond to his visit, but we needed it today. We all can use prayer in our lives. The visits from Pastor Gary and Pastor Soli are a blessing and make us feel we are not alone. Mom slept the rest of the day and night.

Sunday, February 20, 2005

Dear God, we made it through another night. It helps for me to take one hour at a time. I find comfort in Mom's funeral music as much as she does. I feel Mom is at peace now that she is lying so still. God, I told Mom it would not be much longer before she will hear You call her name. Then she can reach her out to her loved ones also. Hear my prayer.

I slept next to Mom's bed last night. I do not know if she will try to get out of bed. This unknown strength makes me not trust her alone. She woke up and screamed once. We got up once for pain pills in the middle of the night. I will be so happy for her when she does not have to take another pill. God has given me so much strength and faith to follow in His path as He leads us through our journey. He has carried me on the days I have asked, when I was troubled and could not walk alone.

I called my girlfriend to see if she could come to Mom's and spend the day with me. She works at the hospital. I had to find someone so I would not be alone with Mom. When she got there, she sat next to Mom's bed and rubbed her hands and arms gently. Mom is weak and having little conversation today. Mom, being Mom, wanted to know about her life. She told her about her job at the hospital and her family. Then she told Mom that her husband was a cook in a restaurant and

Living for the Moment

how he wishes some day he could own his own restaurant. Once again Mom's strength came back. Her eyes lit up, as they always do when she starts talking restaurant business. That was her whole life. Then my girlfriend's phone rang, and it was her husband. He was down and out about having to work for someone else, and we had been talking about this when he called. Mom wanted to talk to him, so she grabbed the phone away from my friend. Mom was so eager to talk that she dropped the glass of pop she was holding and didn't even notice. We cleaned her up and put a new bed spread on while she was on the phone. She didn't even notice that, and she kept talking. She told him on the phone to his follow his dream. She told him how to get started and what to do when he got started. When she hung up, she was ready for a nap, so she told us to go. Her breathing was so bad. She was laboring so hard. It was a hard day seeing Mom like this, but I was so proud of her for talking to stranger and giving him hope.

Darcy came to stay. She wanted me to go home to get some rest. I know she is worried about me. I thank her for that. I cannot leave Mom now. I'm so scared that if I leave, she will die. Mike promised me I could stay, and I want to be here. I promised her I would stay until the end. I promised Darcy I would stay out of the way. My shift is over. Since I'm staying, Bruce and Chuck are on call. I went down into the living room so no one knew I was around. I just wanted to be in the place I have always called home. I slept hard for two hours, until Karen woke me up dancing and clapping her hands, singing, "Hurry, hurry. It's bedpan time. Never know if there's a mess." Darcy, Karen and I used the bedpan. The three of us have really gotten good. We have a roller, holder and wiper. Darcy said we were like a NASCAR team. Mom and Karen were giving orders. I think they were enjoying this too much. Darcy and I were tired, and those two were having the times of their lives.

Karen had come back from being with her daughter and family. Karen and Mom talked about their lifetime of memories. We had a relaxing night. Karen is helping us with Mom. It means a lot having her here.

Brenda Ann Rebelein

Monday, February 21, 2005

Dear God, I'm taking a step back from this situation. I'm going shopping and out for lunch. I will be okay. God, if You call Mom's name while I'm gone, that's okay. I will be just fine.

Darcy and Karen are with Mom today. I went out and had some fun for me. I tried not to think of Mom while I was gone. I did okay. When I get out for a walk, I use some self-discipline. If I think of Mom in that hour that I'm walking, I make myself run. I have learned to take that hour for me. I hate running. They had a fun day, and I did too.

Darcy went home, and Chuck came to stay the night. They have accepted I will not be leaving, so no one mentions it anymore. I have a walking tape here. It was too cold out to walk around the lake, so I went in the living room and put my 3-mile walking tape in. Then here comes Karen and Thelma, Chuck's wife, to watch as they sat on the couch. Of course they were laughing, so I put on a little show. Sheila's computer room faces Mom's living room, and the drapes were open. She called on the phone, and I answered. She wanted to know what I was doing dancing around the room. Karen and Thelma sat on the couch, laughing. "If you're so nosey, come over and find out," I said and hung up the phone. Then I had Sheila on the couch laughing. We are cheap entertainment. Karen thought I had to be my mother's child. Laughter is good medicine and soothes the soul.

Tuesday, February 22, 2005

Dear God, I see us coming closer to the end of our cancer journey. Mom is looking pretty tough. I'm so grateful how we have all pulled together as a support team. We have done a good job with 24-hour care, 7 days a week. I embrace this time.

Today Karen is going home. Mom is too weak to cry. Karen's heart is breaking. She knows it is time to go. This is going to get harder as each day goes by.

Mom woke up earlier and wanted a chicken breast. She doesn't eat anything more than a waffle once in awhile. She called Darcy into the bedroom. "I want a chicken breast. Take it out of the freezer and put it in cold water to thaw it. Season it. Fry it … with one slice of bread." Darcy just looked at her. "Well, go."

104

Living for the Moment

I was sitting at the dining room table laughing. I knew what I would do if I were in the situation. I listened to Darcy and Karen talk about what they could do for Mom when she cannot eat. I listened to them long enough. I was giggling. Finally, I went in the kitchen and told them to get a waffle out. They thought I was nuts. "She wants chicken," they both said.

I got the waffle, fixed up extra butter and syrup, and I gave it to Darcy "Go give it to her, and then tell her it's chicken." Darcy pushed it back to me.

"No way, I will not be involved in your web of lies."

I grabbed it back. "God is a forgiving God. Watch me." I went in the bedroom with Mom's tray with the waffle and hot tea. "Here's your meal you ordered."

She looked down for a minute. "Oh, this looks good. I knew before I died I would make a cook out of Darcy." Mom did not notice. She ate half of her waffle and was done. She thought it was good, but she just was not as hungry as she thought. She went right to sleep.

The nurse was here. Things are progressing. We just need to live one day at a time and not question *when*. I bet the hospice staff hears that at every house they go to. I have tried to get better. They are not God, but they are His helpers. Darcy told the nurse about how we are like the NASCAR team. Even Mom was laughing about that. "I think I'm in trouble. What do you think?" she asked the nurse. She thought Mom had good help. Darcy had to go do payroll for her business, and then she would be back.

The minute Mom knew Karen was getting her things ready to leave, she started to get restless. It was the moment they dreaded. Mom insisted on getting in her wheelchair and sitting at the dining room table with Karen for a few minutes. She did not want Karen to remember her lying sick in bed. They talked a little while. Neither one wanted to move. Mom and Karen said their final good-byes, hugged and kissed, agreed they would be friends forever. It broke my heart to watch Karen walk out that door and not look back. "She is one of my best friends. I got to see her for the last time. Now, I'm ready to die."

I had to add Karen to my journal because she was a big part of Mom getting ready to leave us for a better place. Mom was too weak

105

to cry. It was a sad day for her. Her strong willpower was gone. She wanted to go back to bed.

Bruce is a call away. The four of us kids are going to stay and take care of Mom. The days are getting harder. We do not know one day from the next. We promised Mom that we, her children, would take care of her until the end.

Mom slept all day. I could be alone for a few hours with her sleeping like this. Her breathing is so shallow. If only it would be easy for her to go to sleep and not wake up. A better place is waiting for her.

Darcy came so I could go uptown and have supper with my girlfriend. It was nice to be out of the house. Chuck came and spent the night with me. Mom slept all night, and Chuck said it was because he was here. We are giving Mom backrubs with her being in bed so much of the time now. We don't want her to get bedsores, and we are rolling her from side to side every few hours. Hospice taught us this to prevent the bedsores. They said we are doing a good job keeping her from getting them. We all slept well.

Wednesday, February 23, 2005

Dear God, we face another day. I see Mom is so weak this morning. Her speech is slower and slurred. Help us while we walk together to take care of our mom, grandma, patient, and friend.

It was good to be out of the house for a few hours. Then it was good to be back here. Darcy is coming to stay with Mom. This journey has made us so much closer. This is so hard, seeing Mom like this. I feel powerless. But I have faith God will take care of us. She is not having much conversation with us. She will say a few words now and then. When it is medication time, we say our name and tell her to open her mouth for the medication. I feel that at times this is her way to say goodbye to us as she prepares herself for death.

I went and had coffee with my girlfriend. Darcy stayed with Mom. She told Darcy she would be gone in the next few days unless she went tonight. We just need to stay close.

Bruce's whole family came to spend some time with Grandma. We all know it is getting closer. She is not talking, and that is what is hard for everyone. Mom has never been short on words. There were a lot of

Living for the Moment

tears from knowing that they are losing their grandma and friend. This is part of life. We are lucky to have had her with us so many years. We have had some unforgettable moments.

Tonight was hard. There are many emotions when you are losing a loved one. I have never felt anger. We see her lying so still. It breaks my heart. I wait for her to keep giving me the strength to go on each day. I think I have accepted that this is our plan. We need to keep walking forward.

Darcy had to leave. She has a sick child with the flu. We still have our home lives to live, and when our kids are younger, they count on us. They have to come first. Kids like their mom when they are sick. When we got sick, the first thing we did was call Mom. We knew that in no time we would have homemade chicken dumpling soup to eat. She would never deliver How many kettles of soup did she make once she heard someone had the flu?

Chuck came and spent a few hours with me. He has to work early in the morning. We called Mike to see if he would come and stay with me. We want two people at night with Mom. This is getting hard on all of us. We are getting tired; our nerves are on overdrive. I think we all still like each other. *Smile.* I stare at Mom's church picture on the dining room table right before I have to go help take care of her. This has helped me stay focused. It helps me to face whatever I have to once I go in her bedroom.

She grabbed my arm with force and said, "Please give me pain medication every hour on the hour. My pain is increasing." She closed her eyes and would not talk to me anymore. This is the first time since we have started this journey that Mom has even mentioned her pain level. I called hospice. We got her pain control, and she calmed down. She was restless and could not get comfortable. Increasing her medication helped.

It was good to have Mike here. Josh went and stayed at a friend's house. When Mike got there, he chipped right in. We gave Mom a backrub, and he helped with changing her Depends. She is not leaving the bed anymore. I showed Mike the medications and how much to give. We have to do everything for Mom now. She cannot roll herself. Sometimes she gets strength to help us. We have had to learn to work as a team. During the night, I kept falling asleep. I was so tired and

Brenda Ann Rebelein

worn out. I just wanted to sleep a little while. Mike was checking on Mom all night long.

Thursday, February 24, 2005

Dear God, yesterday was an emotional roller coaster. I feel my waters were tested a few times. Teach me to be a better person. I'm trying not to be scared. Help me, God, as we are so powerless. You always seem to carry me when I'm at my lowest. Keep me strong and hold my faith. Hear my prayer.

Last night Mike and I had plans to take turns staying up with Mom when she was having pain. I kind of slept the night away. She knew who we were this morning. She admitted that some days she does not know everyone. She likes when we say people's names when they come in the room. Mom remembers Mike being in her room last night. "Mike helped me so much last night. He was so good to me. If you need him to stay until the end, it is okay." Mom is not getting company anymore. The word is out that things are progressing. She still gets a lot of calls to see how she is doing. She is worried how we are all doing. She knows we have to be getting tired, but I reassured her we are all doing fine. We can help her the way she helped us for years. This is what love is about, taking care of loved ones. She has loved us unconditionally. I will be so grateful when she starts her new journey. This is no life for her now. We have had fun, but when the fun stops and you cannot enjoy life … we pray God will see her getting tired and know she has suffered enough. I will be ready when God moves us forward. We will keep medication in Mom today. Hospice is helping to keep things under control. Thank God hospice teaches us and walks us through the tough days.

Today was a hard day on Mom. We will survive. I feel bad for her. She is having a lot of pain again. We have had to increase the medication. She acts like she does not know her surroundings this afternoon. Her eyes are rolling in her head. This morning when Mom was so worried about everyone else, she reminded me to thank people for the help they have given her, and for the visits and the calls that always made her day better. She wants me to respect her when things get really bad. "Only my kids see me die." We know now from the last three days that we need Mike here too. He can stay with me during

108

Living for the Moment

the day. If he has to go get things done, he can come right back. We need his help.

She wanted her funeral music on during the day.

Mom asked me to help her die. It breaks my heart to hear this. I want to do something to make things better. It would be easy to give her extra medication, but I'm not God. I will follow His path instead. She is having so much pain; she is rolling around in bed. Her back is hurting her. We have been giving her backrubs, but that has not helped. Her rattle is back; it had gone away. Her breathing is very heavy. I wrote another poem imagining Mom taking her last breath. I have to get my feelings out in writing.

We have two awesome social workers working with us. They are there for us. I'm just so afraid I will fall and not get up. Things are going well for me now. I want to stay strong a little longer. She slept the rest of the day. Her new medication amount has taken effect; she is resting.

We are going to give Mom medication every two hours instead of every four. I fell asleep this afternoon. I overslept on the medication time by a half hour. I cannot tell the difference in Mom.

From now on, we do the medication on time. I learned my lesson. It is my fault she is having this extra pain. Mike had to leave and go to work. I will be alone with Mom for a few hours. I have never been scared to be alone in this situation.

If someone had asked me before if I could do this, I would say no way. You will be surprised what you can do if you have to.

She has been sleeping well again. Mike left, and then Mom woke up. She had some phlegm in her throat. She can get it out, but sometimes she spits it out. This time, it was not coming out. I could not help the phlegm out. I crawled in bed with Mom, trying to turn her on her side. Nothing was working. She was starting to turn colors. I prayed so hard to God to come help us. I thought, *Dear God, do not let Mom die like this in my arms.* I screamed until he heard my prayers and the phlegm worked its way out. She does not have the energy to make it all the way up the throat. This was scary for both of us. My Mom's biggest fear is choking to death. I reassured her again. I was so scared. I thought for a minute, *It is just Mom and me.* Until God reached down and helped us both. The

109

Brenda Ann Rebelein

nurse said she would just pass away peacefully. I do not know if she heard me. She was so happy when she was comfortable again.

Darcy is here with us for the night. Mom is wetting the bed, so we will keep the Depends on her. She has been wearing them a long time already. She was happy when the nurse brought her new underwear. She wanted to share with me.

She is losing her eyesight. I can see she is trying to see me better. She is following voices. Her breathing is bad tonight. She is very raspy and the death rattle is loud. I called the nurse; they think death is around the corner. When I hung up, it was a sigh of relief knowing Mom would be pain-free soon.

I feel that she has been a great trooper through this trip. She has kept us positive. We have laughed at times throughout this journey about how she was doing better than us. She came home from the hospital with a mission to make the best of her time. The jokes she played, some of which we have to keep in the family. She made it fun for people to come and visit, always keeping it in a light mood, being the mom, grandma, family member or friend that we all loved.

Today I have been scared. I know my faith is still good. Like Mom said, today is tough, but we have tomorrow.

She cannot do anything for herself anymore. It takes us two and sometimes three people to do the things we have to do. The medication is getting harder for her to swallow. I feel her body is shutting down.

Giving medication every two hours is helping. She looks so peaceful and comfortable as she rests. Darcy and I are doing shifts taking care of Mom. Sometimes it is hard to get her to take her medication. I do not think she understands sometimes. It is so good not to be alone tonight. Having the support means so much to me. We do not have to walk alone.

Friday, February 25, 2005

Dear God, this is a waiting game now. We are going through the motions. We will be waiting for Mom's body to shut down. She has been through enough, I feel. The battle is almost over. I pray for Mom to keep her pride, dignity, and courage. God, I promise I will be patient, and I will wait with You.

Living for the Moment

Wow ... When I think about what has happened in the last two weeks, it seems like a dream. I think back on that Sunday when Mom had me get phone numbers together. She called a few people to tell them the end was near, that it is harder for her to do things, that she is sleeping more and visiting less. They all knew Mom did not want sadness, so they all handled it well. I bet those four days with Karen were the best four days that they have spent in all the years they have known each other. I remember the moment Karen walked out of her house and Mom looked at me, saying, "I'm ready to die. I never thought I would get the chance to see her again." I will pray for the moment she can finally rest.

We decided it is time to go to liquid medication. She cannot swallow anymore. I still get scared at times from the day she choked, but that day will not control me. With each scheduled medication time, we see Mom getting weaker. It is too hard for her to do this anymore.

Our nurse is here giving Mom a checkup on her progress, and she is getting a bath. We still have the same bath lady, a friend of the family. This has to be hard on her too. She has been a friend for years, and now she has to be professional while she sees her friend slipping away.

We will be doing liquid medications. There is one pain pill that has to be placed in the rectum twice a day 8:00 am and 8:00 pm. They told us that this day would come. Someone would have to step up to the plate to do it. I knew it would have to be me. I have to. She is my mom. She is getting a sponge bath and she is not even moving. It amazes me how they can give a bath, change the hospital gown, roll her, and change the bedding so professionally. And Mom does not know she is being moved. Now that she is wetting herself, they will come to give her a bath daily. Mom has given me so much advice, and soon it will be time to take that advice. I know I need to start preparing myself. I have faith in myself. I will be okay. This journey sometimes seems so long during the rough days. Then at times, it has gone so fast—that was when we were busy having a good time. I just do not want to let her go.

God has Mom here for a reason. It is not for me to question. I will let her go when I know I need too. We have had our time, and boy, it has been fun. People might think something is wrong with me when I say we have had a blast. There was no time for grief; we were having

Brenda Ann Rebelein

a good time. Mom was always doing something, and we never knew if it was the medication or just Mom being Mom.

Mom's pain was starting to come back. Darcy and I thought we could give her an extra little bump. We had seen her suffer with that pain for so long. We decided to do what was marked on the bottle and see how she was in the next two hours. Then we would be guilt free. We went in the bedroom. I told Mom, "It is Brenda. Time for your medication. Open up your mouth nice and wide."

She opened her eyes up nice and wide and up came the index finger. "You are trying to pull a fast one on me you sneaky little shit." Then her eyes closed and she did not move. Darcy and I were both so scared that we wanted to run out of the room. I made Darcy give her the medication. Darcy stayed up all night and gave the medications, and I had to do the rectum pain medication at 8:00 am and 8:00 pm. Mom has not talked in a long time and was unresponsive besides. We just let her know who we are before we give her the medication.

Darcy is so tired, so she went to go lay down. I pulled another fast one. I fell asleep and slept all night. Darcy had to do the shift alone. We were going to help each other, but I just did not wake up. She teased me about what a good nurse I would make. I will have to try and make it up to her. I have to say I have an awesome sister. I'm the lucky one.

I went to help Mike for a few minutes. When we came back, Mom had taken another turn for the worse. Chuck, Bruce and Darcy were taking turns going in her bedroom when we got there. Mom has no control of her body, she cannot talk much, she is wetting the bed, and she cannot tell us what she needs. It breaks our heart to see her so helpless. She was always so strong-willed. She is getting ready for that beautiful place called home.

It is 1:00 am, and I'm on duty. It is time for her medication. She would not open her mouth. They said, if it does not work, you just leave and then come back and try again. She was ready the second time. Every two hours ... the scheduled medications are hard on Mom and us. You get to rest, and then it is time again. I have been doing a lot of praying for help and guidance.

It is late at night. Everyone is getting tired. I have the night shift. I'm ready. Bruce went home for awhile. Darcy is sleeping. Chuck is supposed to be sitting up with me. He is lying on the floor with the

112

Living for the Moment

channel changer under him, and he is snoring. Mom would tell him not to pick on the girls.

I needed help with Mom. She wet the bed. I needed to wash her, put clean bedding on, and put a Depends and a fresh gown on her. I talked out loud to her. I told her I was counting on her to help me. If she could, we would do this together. It was not much, but she could hear me. She helped roll when she could. Her medication is going well now that we are on liquid. I don't think about doing the rectum meds. I just do it.

I held Mom's hand to comfort her. "God will be here soon. Dad will be there waiting for you with open arms." I rubbed her and told her that her friends would be looking for her in heaven. They would be there to show her the way. I could see the emotions in her eyes as a few tears fell. I wiped them away; she gave my hand a squeeze. She opened her eyes. We did not a say word while we looked into each other's eyes. No words needed to be said.

It has been a long day and night. Some of the medications went well, and then others she fought with. I can see Mom's pain is getting worse, but she is not screaming like she was before. She will respond a little at times. We are all doing a good job—the best we know how to do. The end I feel is near. When this is over, I will wait until I see the yellow butterfly come to take my breath away.

Saturday, February 26, 2005

Dear God, thank You for my siblings and Mike. We have all pulled together to support each other. We are all here to hold each other up in our time of need. We are so grateful to have hospice to teach us how to take care of Mom.

Darcy and Bruce came back home. Chuck and I were with Mom. Candy, Mom's hairdresser, brought so much food. She had heard we were doing shifts with Mom, and she wanted to help out in any way she could. Chuck, Bruce and Darcy went to talk to her about how we are not taking anymore visitors because things are progressing. Mom has been a second mother to her. There have been people, so many people, that have been so good to us. How can we ever repay them all?

I'm so glad we kids are here together. It makes it easy when it comes time for medication. The medication is still a trick for us. They change

113

Brenda Ann Rebelein

the medication whenever we need it, and we give her medication every two hours, but there are times when it could be every hour. I will be doing the rectum medication until the end. I told Mom I was sorry for having to do this to her. She laughed, "I bet you are."

Bruce asked if she was in any pain. "No," she said softly.

"Would you lie to us Mom?" he asked.

"Yes," she replied. Her wish is to die on Sunday. We will see what happens. That is tomorrow.

It is nice that she is having a bath every day. There are days she acts like she does not even know that they are there.

We had to call hospice to come to Mom's. Things are out of our control. Mom is in a lot of pain. I wanted to give Mom extra medication, but I could not find in myself the strength to do it. Only because I did not know how much to give. I was fighting with this in my mind. I was standing next to her bed, holding her hand, praying to God to help me. Our earth angel, the hospice nurse, came to take over for me. I was overflowed with relief knowing I did my best. It was time for me to step aside, to let someone in the medical field take over for me. I felt so powerless at the time. I did not want to fail.

I finally lost it. I could not hold my tears back anymore. I went to the living room and cried. They were tears of joy and relief for me. Knowing that I have IBS, and that when my stomach is upset, eating Cheerios takes away some of the pain, God bless my sister, she ran for the Cheerios. Everyone circled around me as I was crying and eating Cheerios. We have been good about comforting each other in our time of need. Mike was at home for the night. I needed Mike for comfort. Bruce asked me if I wanted Mike to come. I sure did. Mike came right away, and he held me while I cried. It felt so good to be in his arms and to know I was safe. Mike knows what to say to me. He knows me better at times than I know myself. I know that is scary. He told me, "You are doing okay. She is your patient now. You wipe your tears, and you will be fine. Soon, she will be your mom again." That was all I needed to hear. Then we had to laugh. It was the first time I had fallen apart. I wanted a bowl of Cheerios which I watered down with my tears. I sent Mike back home again. I reassured him I was fine. I just needed to lean on his strength. It was a blessing to have our nurse take over. I felt a

Living for the Moment

lot better once we got Mom's pain controlled again. The nurse gave her extra medication. We have to give her more at midnight.

Moms' breathing is very heavy tonight. About an hour ago, the wind picked up with such force. The chimes on her deck were clanging and making noise. *Is this her exit to heaven? Are the angels here to give us a sign?* I think we all feel it will be a matter of hours, and Mom will be in heaven to rest in peace.

I made some coffee, and we have so many treats here to eat. We are sitting up to see how things go. No one can sleep anyway. Mom is sleeping peacefully now. One more hour and then we have to give Mom more medication. The nurse said, "After you give the medications, then you all go lay down and get some rest." When she left, I think she knew more than what she was saying. I feel she thinks the end is very near. I'm back to myself, ready to face what happens. I'm just as strong as before, ready to finish my job taking care of Mom. Marvel is my patient, but she will be my mom again when God says her place is ready. I will be so excited for that moment. Time to go get some sleep. Tomorrow may be a big day—a new beginning for all of us.

Sunday, February 27, 2005

Dear God, we all got some sleep. We all know the time is coming closer. Even if we have those tough days, I still get to be with my Mom. This is no life now when you see her suffer. She has been so strong for so long and not showing pain. When it gets unbearable, you know it has to be bad. Thank You for sending those angels through the wind.

It is 12:30 am. How are you supposed to sleep? Chuck and Bruce went home. Darcy and I are here for the night. I have tried. I thought I would write and read my book for a few minutes. Mom is sleeping well. We do not know if we are coming to the final medication. I prayed so hard that she is on her final journey soon. We were told to tell Mom the date and keep repeating it over and over. "Mom, it is February 27, 2005." Darcy and I told her we loved her. She smiled and moaned. We both looked at each other knowing Mom heard us. We know she loves us, too. I will remember that moment forever. God has given us so many special moments to remember, to make us smile. Time will tell

115

Brenda Ann Rebelein

in the morning where we go from here. Darcy is going to stay up. I'm going to try and get some sleep. I will take over in the morning.

Darcy woke me up clapping her hands and screaming loudly, "Up, everyone! Mom is calling for the bedpan. Come before she wets the bed! Hurry, hurry!" Darcy was laughing, and I was in a fog, thinking I was dreaming. I went into Mom's bedroom, and she was talking to Darcy. She had seen people last night. They were coming to get her, and she was suppose to follow them. She was not scared of them. They were so pretty, and they all looked so nice. Medication time had come before I woke up, and Darcy had leaned over Mom's bed to tell her the date. "Mom, it is September 27th." That was our dad's death date. When I woke up, I said the same thing. Darcy was shocked that she had done it, but then I followed her. I could not believe it when she told me what we both had just done at two separate times.

We are still doing the medication every two hours. This morning, Mom only had a small bath because she did not want to be moved. She was not wet, so that helped. We have been good about keeping her clean and dry. It helps giving her back rubs once in awhile, but now she does not want to be touched. She is in a lot of pain when we move her. The nurse called. She is giving Mom more pain medication, and that means more rectum medication. I know I can do this. I have faith in myself. I have a job to do. I will be okay.

We had to call the nurse again. She is on her way. Mom is having a lot of pain in her wrist and back. We gave her back rubs thinking maybe that would help, but it only made it worse. Her eyes are rolling in the back of her head, her breathing is raspy. Her vitals are still good. They say her vitals could be good up until the end. This is so hard at times. She looks right in my eyes and fights to take her medication; we have to slip it inside her mouth. If it does not work, I take a break and try again. We are getting so tired and emotionally drained. We promised Mom we would not let her down. I know we can do this together as a family. We all have great spouses and wonderful kids who are waiting for us at home. We all have been taking that time to call our family. I pray we can last with keeping Mom at home. I do not want to weaken and have her put in a nursing home. I do not want to fail her. We are too close to stop now.

Living for the Moment

Darcy went home to take a shower and to get some rest. Chuck, Bruce and I are together. We think we are looking at one more time, maybe a week. We have learned each patient is different on how they handle the medication. There are so many things to look at. We knew Mom would give them a run for their money. They are having a hard time figuring what works for her. That is our Mom, always leaving people puzzled.

I went to go take a nap for a few minutes. Bruce had gone home. Mike came to sit with Chuck. Mom was talking to Dad out loud. He was telling her to walk with him. She was talking really loud. I still kept sleeping. Then she was talking to a good friend who passed away a few years ago. He was her carpenter. She was hollering at him to fix a window for her. Chuck could not get her to take her medication. Mike came and woke me. Bruce came back then. When I got to Mom's bedroom, Chuck and Mike were by Mom's bed. Bruce was at the head of the bed trying to help them hold Mom down. Mom was pushing those two men away so she could get out of bed. They had all they could do to keep her in bed. Mom looked at Chuck. "What are you doing to me, Chuck? Not you of all people." She was trying to cry, but there was nothing there. I looked across the bed at Chuck. I could see his heart sink. There was nothing I could do for him. They were trying to tell her that she needed to stay in bed for her own sake. She was not listening to them. I tried talking to Mom. She did not know I was there. She kept pushing Chuck and Mike away from the bed, her arms and legs swinging. Where is this strength coming from? It had not been long ago that we could not move her to give her a bath, now she was pushing these two grown men. I thought of her funeral music. I turned it on really loud. She looked puzzled as she turned her head side to side. "Listen, Mom, remember, it is your friend Barb."

"I know her. Oh, that is pretty music."

I was talking to Mom, telling her to listen to her favorite songs. I kept coaching her. Finally, she slowly lay back down. The look Chuck, Bruce and Mike gave me when I turned on the funeral music was priceless. I think they thought I had really lost it. They were shaking their heads. It worked. I had found that trick that we used before during those restless days. In the beginning of the music, Barb says to her daughter Candy, "Well Marvel we hope this works."

Brenda Ann Rebelein

I remember that first day when I tried this trick. I said, "Barb, I hope your right." It has worked ever since. We may wear this tape out and have to order a new one. I called Barb to tell her how much her music has meant to us.

We called Darcy to come to Mom's. We do not know where this goes from here. I think I will write some poems to make myself feel better. I have feelings I do not like. I want them to go away, so I have room only for positive thoughts for my future. Writing has become my escape.

Dear God, I only need a prayer a day. But today I need all I can get. I'm coming back for more. It has been a long day, as you know. So many ups and downs. You can see we are all getting tired. Please, please help this family while we struggle through the day. Mostly, help Mom get comfortable. Help the medical people find the answer they need to treat their patient. She is puzzling them right now. I will take the path You lead me down, just show me the way. We do not know the future. I only take one hour at a time. You know I want time and answers. I need to be patient and wait for a sign. Dear God, I'm so scared as this nightmare is going on forever. I pray to You to please come and put your hand on Mom's head and carry me in my troubled times. In God I pray.

Darcy and Bruce went home. It is Chuck, Mike and me. Josh is staying at a friend's house. I'm so grateful to those that opened their doors to Josh. They treat him like their own. They are letting Josh stay at their homes so Mike can stay at Mom's to help us with taking shifts, watching Mom, helping with medications or rolling her for backrubs. Mike has started taking the role of a caretaker, and he has become part of our support team. We are doing medications like before, every two hours. I need faith not to be scared while we are reintroducing our enemy drug that we had before when Mom got that bad reaction. I have faith that our medical staff knows what they are doing. I will do as I'm told and accept this change. I need to remember change is good. I have written a few poems. It has helped.

Tonight I read some angel stories to Mom. She is resting again. She does not move or talk to us. Children have been a big part of Mom's life. I read a story to Mom out of the angel book about a sick mom who lost her daughter to an illness. She was her mom's angel. She sent a doctor to her mom's house to save her life. Mom has been unresponsive

118

all afternoon. When I was done reading that story, she said, "Isn't that something." I knew then that she had heard me. I tried to get her to talk to me but that was all she would say. I have to be grateful for what I had just received. Darcy came tonight. I told her what happened; she was amazed. Darcy is reading the Bible to Mom.

Mom had her bath. We help the bath lady because it is a lot for one person. We have to roll Mom from one side to the next. She is not helping us anymore. The bath lady leaned over and wanted to know if Mom wanted her teeth cleaned. "Only if you promise me the kids will not see." She is talking once again. This has been a joke of ours for years. Mom would not let us see her without her teeth. She promised Mom she would show us out of the room and close the door. When we came in, Mom wanted to know who was in the house. We told her the bath lady, the nurse and we kids and Mike. Mom got very upset thinking there were other people in the house besides her kids. She got angry. We assured her we kept her promise. Mom said, "This is my life. I do not want people seeing me when I look tough. I want to be remembered as being happy and looking good, not like some old lady who is dying. It's my life." We have to honor her wish. I have told everyone to take this as the last time they will see her, so they have that final moment with her. What do you do? Respect the person that is dying or think about the person who is left behind? I do not know what the best answer is. My family has told me I have been bad about being Mom's protector. We have changed roles. I'm the adult, she is the child. I'm doing what I feel I need to do and want to do. She is my only mom.

Monday, February 28, 2005

Dear God – We are facing another day. I do not understand any of this. I have never gone through this before. When Dad was sick, he was in the Vets hospital. He had a lot of things wrong with him. Having him at home was not an option. I'm praying for Your guidance. We have Mom resting. You are carrying me through this ordeal. I cannot walk alone. I need You with me. I need to remember each day is a gift from You. I need to embrace it with open arms.

It is Chuck, Mike and I here. We gave Mom her medication. It takes three of us to help Mom. We have to give her the liquid medications

Brenda Ann Rebelein

in an eyedropper. Then two people have to roll her, then I have to do the medication in the rectum. At 5:00 am, Mom went wild. She was doing a lot of chatting out loud. She was not hurting anything; she was not trying to get out of bed. She was chatty on and on. It lasted four hours before she calmed down. She finally fell asleep for a couple hours. When she woke up, she was talking to me. She wanted me to order Krispy Kream doughnuts for her funeral. Does she know what that would cost? She wanted me to make the call right in her room so she could listen. I know I have become an actress, with the roles I have taken here. I pretended I was talking to someone and ordered 250 Krispy Kream doughnuts for her funeral. She was happy that was settled. She told Chuck to take care of me. Chuck and Bruce always had to take care of us girls. I tried to tell her she could help me right now if she would rest for me. She looked at me like she was looking right through me. She went back to being chatty.

I'm getting so emotionally and physically drained. I have done all the medication since yesterday. I do not tell anyone that I'm tired or they will send me home. They have all accepted I will not leave unless I want to go for coffee. I promised I would stay until the end, and that is a promise I mean to keep. We talked Bruce into going home. We would call if things change. If he wants to come back to see how things are going, that is okay, too. We talked Darcy into going home for awhile. She could have a break and come back refreshed. She also has young girls at home. They are at the age when they need Mom, too. They want their mom here to help Grandma, but they also want their mom at home. Josh is having a lot of fun being with his friends. We are lucky he has been given places to stay so Mike and I can be here. Then when Mike is home, they do their guy things. I wonder if they have three food groups: call out pizza, hamburgers or chicken.

When I feel myself slipping, I go write another poem. I want to stay focused on my job as a caretaker and yet get some rest. I know that I need rest. I have been taking that time. I cannot help but ask now, how much longer? My prayer is for guidance and the path we will be going. I will be holding my head up knowing that I'm doing my best.

I think Mom's lungs are filling up. She will talk once in awhile to us but not hold full conversations. Mom kicked Chuck, Bruce and me out of her room. We watched to see what she was going to do. We did

Living for the Moment

not want her to try and get out of bed. She crossed her arms real tight. She was talking to God. She was ready for him to come to her. She wanted him to hear her prayer. She did not want to suffer anymore. She slept a few minutes.

Today was a hard day for Chuck and me. We could not settle Mom down. She wanted to get out of bed; she was pushing us, talking out of her head, spitting her medication out. This went on from 5:00 am to 3:00 pm. It was a nightmare day. God will only give us what we can handle. He must have a lot of faith in us today.

Darcy and Bruce came and took over for us. I think Chuck grabbed his boots and left. It was a tough one. I went down in the living room and slept by Mom's nice warm fireplace. I slept hard for three hours. Darcy called hospice. We may have to put Mom in the hospital in a hospice room, or we can have hospice volunteers come and stay with Mom in three hours shift from 8-4. They do not stay at night time. We are all getting so tired and drained. We will see how it goes. I do not know how much longer we can take care of Mom when we have days like today. I get sad thinking we cannot do this. Mom made us strong. I want to cross the finish line of this cancer journey knowing that wishes do come true.

Darcy is doing all the medication tonight. I will just have to get up to do the rectum medication at 8 and 8 as directed. Mom is in a coma. She is having apnea really bad tonight. Darcy and Bruce took over. I slept all night long in the living room next to the warm fireplace. Mom was so proud of the fireplace she had built when she remodeled her home.

Chapter 6

New Beginnings For Us All

March 2005

We are facing the seventh month in our cancer journey. I take one hour at a time, and that is okay for me. I feel so much better knowing that I do not have to leave and go home and come back for another shift. When I leave here, Mom will be making her safe journey to heaven to be with God. I was feeling before like *she can not leave me.* Now that things are progressing, I see her slipping away. It is okay. I will be fine. I will miss her, but she taught me not to be selfish and to let the chips fall where they may. This cancer journey gave me more than I ever dreamed of. I learned so much about myself. I can do any thing I want if I put my mind to it. I will succeed. You have so many feelings when you go on a cancer journey. It changes every day. One feeling I'm glad I did not hang onto was anger. I was angry one day, only for a few hours, when Mom was having a bad afternoon. I was angry at the cancer. I knew that anger is a killer, so I removed those thoughts with compassion. I sit by her bedside knowing there is no other place I would want to be than right here. I'm so grateful for so many things that could make this happen. As I live one hour at a time, it is about keeping a positive attitude no matter what stepping stones we cross. The children and grandchildren have all received Moms' strength.

Tuesday, March 1, 2005

Dear God – Thank You for calming things down for Mom. She deserves the best. We have had the surge of energy that hospice talked about. She has had a lot of extra surges, but this one was different. It is time for her to rest in peace until her room is ready. We are living for the moment.

Bruce and Darcy let me sleep through the night. We talked about putting Mom in the hospital for a week. Chuck has a full-time job trucking. Bruce, Darcy and I own businesses. It would give everyone

Living for the Moment

a break to get caught up on some rest. I need to realize we have done our best. It kills me to think of Mom having to leave her home to go lie in a dark hospital room all alone. We have made it this far, so I want to hang in there a little longer. Yesterday, our hospice nurse talked to us about having hospice volunteers come to Mom's from 8:00 am - 4:00 pm. The volunteers only stay during the day. I can rest during the day. Then Chuck, Bruce, Darcy and Mike can come and stay with me at night. I will give it a try. She said just try it one day, then we will go from there. There are going to be three ladies a day coming in. The first one 8:00 - 11:00, the second one 11:00 - 2:00, and the last one is 2:00 - 4:00. They will come and sit in Mom's bedroom. They will comfort her, talk with her, and rub her hands to let her know she is not alone. They can bring a past time—a book to read, knitting, or any preference. It is quiet time for the patient and caretaker. They do not give medications. I will still have to do that. The person who is leaving at 8:00 am, and who stayed with me last night, can help me with the morning meds. Then at nighttime they are here any way. Getting rest for two hours straight during the day sounds like heaven. It is hard for me to leave Mom's side. If I want to keep Mom at home, I have to get some rest. Mom is so still and peaceful. The medication is every two hours.

The nurse is calling every day to see how things are going. Things are a lot more peaceful. Mom has the death rattle really bad, and she is snoring loudly. We had our first volunteers here, and one had lost her husband to cancer. She had hospice in her home four weeks. The next one lost her husband to cancer. She had hospice for six weeks. The last one lost her husband to cancer. He had it for four years, and she had hospice five months. I had a call from the hospice office. They said the ladies that were here today would be happy to come back tomorrow if I want. I had to agree it was nice to go and hide for two hours. I did not think this is a long time, but when you go on not much sleep, that is a long time just to unwind. It left me with a warm feeling. They were so caring and soft spoken; they always had a warm hug to give.

Tomorrow is another day I can get some rest while the volunteers are here. The bath lady was here. Mom did not talk or move while she was getting a bath. She lay so still. The nurse was here. She was surprised how much Mom had failed since yesterday. Mom is doing a lot of chatting. This went on for two hours straight. She was talking

Brenda Ann Rebelein

about being in a motel with a fancy lady and she was too good to go to the front deck. Then she made some mimicking sounds, and then she was talking about her childhood out on the farm. She was rattling on and on. She was also talking about babies. I would have thought she would have gotten tired of talking. I was able to rest for two hours, and then it was time for me to give her medication. I told her my name, the date, and the time. We've been giving her water from a dropper.

We have decided to start doing shifts each night so we can get some rest. Bruce had the day shift. Tonight, Chuck's shift is 8:00 pm - 12:00 am. Mike is 12:00 am - 4:00 am, and I will be 4:00 - 8:00. I will still do medication every two hours. It is so hard seeing Mom like this. It has helped me stare at her church picture and stay focused so I'm ready to do the job that needs to be done. No matter how touchy it gets, I would not want to be any other place. It makes sense to do shifts rather than sitting around and all of us getting tired. It helps that we all work together as Marvel's team.

Wednesday, March 2, 2005

Dear God – I pray for all of us as we start another new day. I pray for closure soon for Mom. We are close to being in her final stage of cancer. We know that cancer can kill. We did not know how strong we all could be. We have all gone out of the comfort zone. My brothers are doing things most men would never do for their mothers while doing their stay of shifts. Darcy works full time at her business, plus her book keeping jobs and taking care of Mom full time. Mike, being a son-in-law, is stepping up to help us get medication for Mom and taking shifts so we can sleep. For me, it's being a caretaker who never leaves her patient, making sure Mom can stay home ... Today I will make a start in letting go.

Chuck and Mike did a great job last night. I did the medication every two hours. This is a good idea with the shifts running. It must have been my idea. Mom was restless early this morning. I had Chuck and Mike help roll her side to side. I gave her a back rub and a full body massage. This seems to help when I think about the days she has been in bed. She always gets extra energy. We keep waiting for maybe one more surge. That last one was the big one though.

The volunteers are here from 8:00 - 4:00 so I can rest. I will still do the medication every two hours as planned. The bath lady and the

Living for the Moment

nurse are here. Mom is cold and clammy. It is weird that the only one Mom will respond to is the nurse. I think in Mom's mind she has said goodbye to me. I thought I would be devastated when I read that in the hospice book. It is okay, we have had our time. We knew that this was coming. I have taken baby steps, and when I thought it was time to step up my feelings, I did that. So when we passed another stage, I was ready. Each shift, I pretend it is my last day with Mom, so when we start another shift it is only another plus for me.

Mom told the nurse she thought we were over-medicating her. We are giving her enough medication to kill a horse. She informed Mom we were giving her what she had prescribed, so it was okay. When they left Mom, she was doing a lot of chatting. This went on for hours again. She is in her own world now. I sit by her bed letting her know that I'm near. I do not think she understands. We have had a lot of good talks in this bedroom. I have found out more about my Mom in the last few months then I did in all these years being her daughter.

This afternoon, when it was medication time, Mom fought it. I came back a few minutes later. She was ready for me. She opened her eyes, and I talked to her about the date and time, the weather, and the people that called and asked about her. She smiled, and she looked me right in the eye as she put up three fingers in the air. "Can I please have three cookies, or crackers will do. I promise I will be good." This broke my heart. I knew she could not have anything. She is not eating or drinking. We are using those mouth sticks to wet her mouth. I tried to let her down gently knowing food is not possible. She either fell asleep or she detached herself from me. I will never forget the powerless feeling when Mom only wanted a cookie and there was nothing I could do for her but pray. It has been days since she had a waffle. We did try giving her food when she was talking, but she kept gagging and we finally knew her waffle days were over.

When Mike was leaving this morning, he went to Mom's bed. "Marvel, it is Mike. I have to go to work and get Brenda more clothes, and then I will be back. Okay?"

"I know who you are. I'm not dumb." She spoke real loud. Then she was silent for a few minutes, and she cleared her throat. "I hope I die before you get back. If I'm still alive, come back and give me shit S-H-I-T shit."

We had to laugh. Mike and I looked up at the doorway and there stood a new hospice volunteer. "Hello, come in. I'm Brenda, a daughter, my husband, Mike, and this is my mom, Marvel." We were all still giggling.

"Well, at least we know your mom can still spell," our new earth angel said. Mike left, and the volunteer sat by Mom's bed. I went to get caught up on some needed rest. Mom did not need medication for the next two hours.

Darcy and I are here for the night. Mom is so restless and chatty. She talks too loud. The positive thing is she is not trying to get out of her bed. She looks so tough. She is still my mom, and she will always be that beautiful women I love. The cancer or drugs are doing so much to her mind. She is picking at her clothes. We are seeing our mom melt away to nothing. She asked me who I was tonight. I smiled at her. "My name is Brenda. I'm here to take care of you tonight." She fell right to sleep as I held her hand.

Mom was chatty through the night and while taking her gown off. It is good to have two or three people here to stay together to take care of Mom. It has been good for us to be together as Mom's kids to help her in her final days. We take turns checking on her and fighting over the TV. Thelma and Mike have been keeping us in food. We get treats from Darcy and Jeremy's Meat Market. Family and friends are coming in with meals to serve us. The only visitors we have are hospice.

Thursday, March 3, 2005

Dear God – We are so tired. Will we be able to keep going? I know You are only giving us what we can handle. Does this mean I'm strong? I'm so grateful my family is so understanding and is letting me have this time with my mom and siblings. My gratitude for Mike helping out will always be remembered. I want to stay strong, but each day it is getting harder. Please carry us as we are coming to the end our of Mom's cancer journey. Hear my prayer.

Darcy had the shift from 10 pm-3 am. She was awake all night with Mom. What an early morning I had. Darcy woke me up at 3 am so I could start my shift. Mom had vomited blood through the night, and then it turned into something that looked like a coffee ground mixture. Darcy warned me that when I saw her, she would just have a

Living for the Moment

sheet on. She kept taking her hospital gown off and was picking at the bedding. She had been chatty the whole time I was sleeping. I never heard a word. Darcy is so tired. I wish she had woken me up to help her through the night so she would not have had to walk alone. We all know how good it feels to get some rest. She did not want to bother me since I never leave Mom's home.

Darcy went to the bedroom to get some rest. I sat next to Mom's bed. She was chatty for seven hours straight. It was so hard to see this. It is a stage we have to get through, so I have to accept what is happening. I feel Mom is not suffering. She is not having the pain she was having before. She is bringing her fingers to her mouth to feed herself. Oh, how I wish I could go get her some mashed potatoes and stewed tomatoes. She has been doing this a long time as I sit by her bed. She mumbles that she needs a spoon. I thought it could not hurt anything if I can watch her closely. I put the spoon in her hand and talk to her. She started feeding herself. Her eyes are staying closed the whole time. She is still chatty and feeding herself. Then Mom started talking so I could understand her. "Go get some warm plates before my food gets cold. Let's get this party served quickly." I walked away from the bed without thinking, turned around, and came back to Mom's bed and opened my hands to her. "Here, Mom. Here are your warm plates." She took them from my hands. In the restaurant business, we always served food for our parties on warm plates. She was busy in bed serving her last party. I told her the people enjoyed their food. She was glad to hear that. I want to cry when I think of all the good parties we had together. The past is the past, it is a memory. I'm just lucky I got to be here to serve this party with her. I have to remember, no tears. Mom has taught me to be strong. I will succeed with this job I have to do. I feel Mom knew she had to prepare me to take care of her. She had faith in me that I could do this for her and myself. I think about what I have, not what I want. I will always remember her smile and positive attitude.

I called hospice to see if we could do something different instead of giving Mom medication every two hours. It is hard on her and us as caretakers. What would we do without hospice? They will be taken care of when this is over with. That is one wish of Mom's we know will come true. We would not still be in Mom's home without hospice.

127

Brenda Ann Rebelein

I do pray hard that we can fulfill her dream that we will be here until the end.

Mom is lying so still. She is done cooking; the party went well. We had three volunteers come from hospice today. When our first lady came into Mom's bedroom, she went right to the bed and held Mom's hands and introduced herself to Darcy, Mom and me. She told Mom she would be with her for the next few hours. She was one of the first ladies to get hospice started. I can see the comfort she was giving Mom as she talked so softly. Mom lay there so still. She talked about her family and her past cooking experiences. We talked about the cancer journey. I talked about my feelings. I like to write things out. The volunteer was talking about how we all have feelings to let out and to not hide them. Mom spoke up with such command, "Don't hold feelings inside. It is wrong, wrong, wrong." We all had a look of surprise on our faces. Mom, still being Mom, was giving me advice. We smiled at each other. Mom went right back to sleep.

Early this morning, Mom had folded her hands and prayed to God to come and take her. She was ready to go to a better place. I think she might die of starvation with no food and no water. It has been seven days since she has had food and five days without water. We are still giving her drops of water in her mouth with a dropper.

Darcy and I went for a walk. Caretakers need to take care of themselves so they can take care of the loved one. This has been the hardest thing for me to learn. Bruce stayed with Mom. We are giving medication to Mom so we can get some rest at nighttime. It has helped doing shifts at night so someone can sleep before someone else takes over. It is March 3rd. Will Mom make it until her birthday, March 16? It sure would not surprise any of us if she would be here. She made me promise no matter what is happening we would all go for her birthday and have a good time celebrating her life. One day at a time.

Karen called from Arizona. She was crying. The last thing Mom said to her was. "Watch out for the yellow butterfly." Karen explained to me that the trailer park they live in is picture perfect. The homes are all the same. Karen had gone for a walk this morning. A neighbor called to her to come in and have a cup of coffee with her. Karen had never walked around there before. She cut across on the road to get to this lady's trailer, and there in the middle of the road was a yellow

Living for the Moment

butterfly on a stick. This happened the same time we were having problems with Mom being restless. What does this mean? Is it that we are all tired and losing our minds? What a beautiful moment for Karen. She wanted me to whisper in Mom's ear. "Mom, Karen received her yellow butterfly." She was so still as she received her news.

We all were scared to reintroduce the drug Mom a bad reaction to before. Hospice taught us not to be afraid. We need to face things head on and try new things as we go down this journey. We have to have faith in them. They know what they are doing. They have taught us that this medication is something we need to try again.

Friday, March 4, 2005

Dear God – Good morning. It is really quiet and very early in the morning. I have so many blessings today. I pray for strength as we step into another day. I need to try and be the person I was before this disease took over my life. When looking for a blessing, I do not have to look very far. Today, I will be blessed with a sunny day that helps us through this journey.

It is my shift now. The shift is running from 12:00 am - 4: 00 am. Mike will relieve me at 4:00 am. I'm sitting next to Mom's bed for my comfort. I can see and touch her. Soon, I will not get to do this. She has been telling Dad to come and get her. She is waiting. She wants to get out of bed. She keeps asking for someone to help her. She keeps repeating, "Help me, help me." It breaks my heart, I feel so powerless and empty. It was not so long ago she was this strong, well taken care of, independent women who had fun no matter where she went. If she wanted to do something or take off in her big motor home, she just planned the trip. Now she can not do anything for herself, her face is starting to sink in. She is resting again.

Mike is with me. I went to have a nap since Mom is resting. It seems it can change from one minute to the next, so we have to get rest when we can. Mom woke up with so much pain. She was screaming and rolling, then she would scream if we touched her to help her get more comfortable. The nurse is coming every day with the bath lady. The hospice office called. They are on their way. Thank God, the help is coming. We just have to hang on a few minutes longer. Mom rolled enough that she is lying sideways on the bed. She is trying get out of

129

Brenda Ann Rebelein

bed. Mike used to work in a nursing home, so he knows how to handle situations like this. She pushed herself up and fell back in bed. Mike was talking to Mom, trying to get through to her to stay where she was. Help is on the way. I kept running to the deck to see if the nurse was coming. Then as quickly as she pulled up, she drove away. Mike held Mom in his arms as she hung over the bed. When we tried to put her back in bed she would scream. Mike held Mom for what seemed like forever. I will never forget what he did for my mom to keep her safe, and how he helped her with her pain. We got pillows behind her to help with the pain. He kept promising her he would make things better for her. She was getting heavy for him, she is dead weight. Then our miracle nurse came back. She had forgotten her medical bag at home—the first time in all her years she has done that. We were glad to have her take over. Mike held Mom for 25 minutes. We told her Mom is in too much pain and we could not move her. "Well, we have to count to three and let's move her back in bed," our nurse ordered. Mom screamed, but she was safe back in bed. She gave Mom some medication. She waited a few more minutes and then gave her some more.

Finally I could see Mom getting more relaxed. I could see the pain was leaving her.

When things calmed down, she changed Mom's medication. We are still keeping the drug we are scared of. It is all about having faith in our nurse. When she was leaving, she heard Mom scream; she dropped her bag and ran in the bedroom. She gave her more medication. She promised that if we needed help, to call and she would come back right away.

Mom cried and moaned all day. I prayed to God that Chuck, Bruce, or Darcy would not come to see Mom suffer so. She had tried dying in my husband's arms, screaming to be taken to heaven. I thought she was going die in his arms today. We finally got Mom's back pain in control, but she cried and moaned until 7:00 pm. She is sleeping well now. Bruce and Darcy are here to give me a break. Mike went home for the night. Her breathing is very shallow. I pray so hard we are getting closer to Mom's new journey.

Dear God – I'm going to rest and clear my mind now that things have calmed down. Thank You for letting me have Mom so many years. She has been a great family

Living for the Moment

*member and friend to us all. She has been our rock. I promised her we would all
stay together. Take her hand and lead her to the light. God, hear my prayer. Time
for some rest. Help me take care of me.*

Saturday, March 5, 2005

*Dear God – Thank you for the good rest I received. I'm ready to face my day.
Bless you for giving my mom a pain-free moment. She is sleeping comfortably. Put
your hand on her head for her final hours and carry me through my day. In God
I pray.*

While my shift started at 12:00 am, I was ready for duty at 11:30
pm. Mom always taught me to come to work early and always come
prepared to work. We gave Mom her medication, and she did not move.
We slid her medicaion in her mouth in droppers. Darcy went to bed
until 8:00 am. Medication time.

Darcy woke Mom up at 8 am for her medication time. "Mom, it is
Darcy. Do you have any pain?" Mom did not open her eyes. She shook
her head. "No pain." Darcy and I smiled. Finally after all those hours
earlier she has no pain. We had been giving her medication every two
hours. She would not respond to us when we talked.

We have kept Mom's promise not to have any company since she
told me to stop the company. Everyone had their goodbyes with Mom.
If they wanted to see her one more time, I had to tell them that she
is slipping and to remember the last time they were with her. Then I
remind them of the good time they had laughing and talking about
the good old days. Let that be your lasting memory of Mom. It is hard
to know what is best. It is hard for the person who is passing away and
hard for the person who is left behind. The grandchildren had been
here for their finally moments. I knew my daughter Monica's feelings
about her grandma. She was working two days of double shifts at the
nursing home when we stopped the visitors. She did not get here to say
goodbye to grandma. She was unhappy with her final goodbye. I had
told her to talk to the social worker, and they would help her with her
feelings. I just wanted her to feel better about the situation.

Darcy and I have been reading boxes of angel books for the last
couple days. I walked into the bedroom one night as Darcy was sitting
next to Mom's bed looking sad, reading an angel book. I asked her what

131

Brenda Ann Rebelein

was wrong. She wanted an angel to come to see her. I had to laugh. I told her "Sorry, angels do not come on command." We are thinking about and reading about angels. We decided, since Mom is sleeping well, we should get some rest ourselves.

I was on duty, so I went to sleep in the dining room in the recliner so I could still see into Mom's bedroom. Darcy went into the other bedroom and shut the door. I fell asleep. I woke up to Mom screaming. I ran to her bedroom. Monica was standing by her bed. I did not know if I was dreaming or this was really happening. "Grandma, it is Monica. I just want to tell you that I love you. We will all be okay." Mom opened her eyes and smiled. She put Monica's face into her hands. "My Monica, my angel. It's so good to see you. I love you. Stay happy and take good care of my house." Mom had not raised her hands in days because she had had so much pain. Now she was holding Monica's face in her hands. They were hugging and saying their final goodbyes. I feel that I'm dreaming.

I left the bedroom to go the kitchen to get the medication that had to be chilled, and then I went back into the bedroom to finish preparing the medication for what was scheduled. This all happened within a few minutes. "Mom, I'm sorry I had to say goodbye." I keep working on my medications thinking this is not happening. Monica was in the hallway leaving. Darcy came out of the bedroom to see what the commotion was. She saw Monica and she did not know what to say. Darcy walked back into the bedroom. I was filling medication. "Thank you, God. Thank you, God. I have a voice. Thank you, I can talk. Hello, hello. I have no pain." Mom was talking real loud. She hollered for us to come to her. She wanted a group hug. Darcy, Monica, Mom and I hugged. We turned, and Monica was gone. We were enjoying the moment. Mom had not talked for a long time. Darcy and I looked at each other. Then Darcy went to the bedroom. I sat next to Mom. She went to sleep right away. I had so many mixed feelings about what Monica had just done. Then I was thinking, *Was she really here or did I dream this?*

After a few minutes, Darcy came to Mom's bedroom. We both were confused. We went into the dining room to talk. Did we really see Monica here? We are so tired, our days are all rolled into one. Have we been reading so many angel books that they are coming out in us. We got to laughing; we were crying. I called over to Sheila's house next

132

Living for the Moment

door. Monica has been spending a lot of time over there. I talked to Monica. Yes, she had been there. She apologized for not respecting our wishes, but she needed this goodbye. After we talked, I hung up. Darcy and I talked. We were okay with what happened. It was just so funny; we thought we were losing our minds. We do have to think of the ones who are left behind. We are so focused on Mom's wishes. This worked out okay. The truth will come out some day, so everyone knows we hope everyone understands. It was a moment the four of us will never forget. Darcy and I decided to give the angel books a rest.

I have been thinking about the situation ealier this afternoon with Monica. At first I was angry. Then I think of the smile on Mom's face when she was saying goodbye to Monica. She then went to right to sleep like nothing had happened. Mom was so peaceful. The glow on Mom's face was priceless, and it is a moment I know that I will never forget. It might have been wrong for Monica to disrespect us. Things happen for a reason. It was a chance Monica took. We have to think of the ones that are left behind. We all needed to be satisfied with our final goodbye. I know Darcy and I have forgiven her. I pray everyone in the family forgives her. Things happen for a reason.

We woke Mom up for medication, and she needed changing again. We cleaned her up and changed her bedding. Before we could not touch her; she would cry in pain. Now we can move her. The medication is working well. Hospice does miracles when we have bad days.

Sunday is coming. We think of that each week. She wants to pass away on a Sunday. Mom has been sleeping well. She got a bath from hospice like she does each day. Once we got her cleaned up, she vomited blood until it was coffee-like. They say it does not hurt. She may have been bleeding internally for a month. Mom asked for Mike. She said he would take care of her. She remembered Mike holding her for a long time. She has not talked for a long time. She is holding a full conversation. We can not believe how much she is talking.

Pastor Gary was here. It is a nice warm feeling after he has been here. The visits from Pastor Soli and Pastor Gary mean so much to us. When Mom was doing well she would make them feel better, too, when they left, so we all help each other in our time of need. They have words to make it all turn into something good. It has been a long week.

Brenda Ann Rebelein

Tomorrow we face another Sunday. Will Mom's wish come true? Will Sunday be her passing day?

This afternoon, Mom is vomiting a lot of blood. This has gone on all weekend. Mike is with Darcy and me. We have prayed so hard that this is coming to an end for Mom really soon. I love the support team hospice has taught us to be. This is making us better people to help others.

I wrote poem's during my shift:

Sunday, March 6, 2005

Dear God — I slow myself down as I begin my shift. Mom is doing a lot of coughing, To me, God, it sounds like her lungs are filling up. I pray this is the end of our journey for Mom's sake. Keep us all safe in your arms and let us feel the warmth of You as we face another day. In God's name I pray.

Mom is still hanging in there. The death rattle is really loud. I can smell death in her bedroom. I'm not afraid; this is my mom. She was doing so much more coughing when I went to go lie down after my shift. I thought it will be a blessing if they wake me up and tell me she is gone. Bruce is with Darcy. I need some rest.

I was sleeping for two hours and Bruce and Darcy woke me. Mom was screaming for me. It was time to serve another party with warm plates; I sat next to her bed telling her how good the party was going. It was nice using warm plates, her customers were satisfied. Bruce and Darcy were just shaking their heads. Mom had served our last party together, the memories will last forever. Finally the party was served, and Mom fell asleep.

Chuck and Mike came to be with us. We had to set up more schedules as we live day to day. Mom woke up a few hours later, she was very restless and agitated. She wants to sit up to get the blood out of her mouth. It has helped giving her water to help spit it out. This went on for a long time. The good thing is when there are three of us to do this together. Once we got the blood out, we had to give her extra pain medication to get her settled down. She asked us what was wrong with her. We told her she was dying, we were waiting for her room to be ready in heaven. We reassured her we all would be okay and that we would take care of each other. She was so confused. Mike folded

134

Living for the Moment

Mom's hands together and told her to pray to God that she was ready for a better life. Mom folded her hands real tight and closed her eyes. "God, come and get me. I'm suffering. Help me, help me, God." She slowly relaxed and went to sleep.

We called Pastor Soli to come and see Mom. When he came, he told us he sees the difference since he was here the last time. He agreed it would be soon that Mom would be meeting her maker. We have had so many false calls, and she has had so many bursts of energy, we think she will have more. Now is the time to face that Mom's journey is almost over.

Darcy went home for awhile. Bruce, Chuck, Mike, and I were at Mom's. When Darcy came back, they wanted Mike and I to go out for a malt. They would watch Mom; she was sleeping good any way. It had been a long time since I had left the house besides going for a quick walk once in awhile. Mike and I went for a malt and went to get a few things we needed. It was nice to be away from the house. It was nice for a few minutes not having to worry about medication time or seeing if Mom was wet and needed changing.

The sun is shinning. It is a perfect day. When we got back, I was so relaxed I was ready for a nap. I took the cot out on Mom's deck, and I fell right to sleep. I covered my whole head. With us living in a small town, everyone knows everyone. Today was a steady stream of walkers going around the lake. They saw me sleeping on the cot covered up. People were staring, thinking it must be Mom because the word is out how bad she is. If Mom was up and about, she would be laughing. They teased me when I woke up about how many people were looking at me. It was the best nap I have had in a long time. I slept for three hours. Sometimes your body says enough is enough. Mom slept well the rest of the night.

Monday, March 7, 2005

Dear God: Mom is starting to suffer. Please guide her to a better place we call home. She has been good to so many people. I feel she deserves peace. She is calling Dad and praying to You. I feel she is finally ready to give up control. I know we are ready to let her go. I know I have been trying to rush You and not let You do your work. Please forgive me.

Brenda Ann Rebelein

It is time for the midnight shift. Darcy went to bed after we gave the medication. Mike will take over at 4:00 am. I do not know who will be here with me tomorrow as we will live one day at a time. For me personally, I do one hour at a time. Sometimes this feels like a bad dream. I know this is reality because I can feel the pain. It has been ten days since Mom's had any food. She has only drops of water.

The nurse and bath lady come at the same time each day. It is so nice to see them come every day. They always give us positive feedback that we are doing a good job. We need to hear that right now. We will have the volunteers coming back to sit with Mom so I can rest during the day but still give the medication when needed. Then Darcy, Chuck, Bruce and Mike can work during the day. We do not know how much longer Mom has.

It is 3:30 am. I try to not get scared at times. I feel so bad when I question God's work. It seems each day is the same; they are all rolled into one. This seems to go on and on. I pray for the moment when Mom's room is ready and she can go in peace. We have all been telling Mom how much we love her and that we will be okay. I pray for the day she can become the carefree yellow butterfly. One day Megan read a book from hospice for kids. "Grandma has it all wrong. She will become a dragonfly not a butterfly." We had to laugh. The things kids say.

It is bath time and the nurse is here. Mom's vitals are still good. They say they can be good until the end. We have three volunteers coming from hospice. I call them our earth angels. They are such nice caring people and have walked in our shoes at one time. I remember how scared I was to let go and have them come and sit with Mom so I could get some rest. I know now it is okay to need the help. I do not have to walk alone. Now I look forward to those two hours to rest. It makes me feel special when I think about our nurse saying, "Let's just try it for a day, see how it goes." She knew that this is would be something I needed, I just needed that little push.

Today Mom looked at me. "I wish I had a million dollars to give to be able to sit at my dining room table to have lunch with you one last time. I would serve liver and onions." Then she closed her eyes. I hate liver and onions. I do not know if this was still her humor or she was thinking of cooking her favorite meal. She tried for years to get me to like it. That day she cooked it for Candy and Chuck, she told me to quit

Living for the Moment

being a baby and learn how to cook good liver and onions. That was my last cooking lesson.

Mom is really restless today. She is picking at her gown and trying to take the bedding off. We do not have a comforter on her any more; she only uses a sheet. Today was a bad day for Mom. She was gurgling a lot today; the rattle is still there. She is not soaking the bed as much as she was before. I know that is another sign we were to look for. Her body is shaking. I want to cover her up, but she just pulls the blankets off. If we can leave a sheet on, I'm happy. We are up to two thousand milligrams a day to keep her comfortable. We are still at the two hours medication schedule. She has been chatty for hours again. Her eyes are open, but it is like she is sleeping. She is trying to vomit up blood, but nothing is coming out. The days seem to be getting so long. I will be having volunteers coming in every day this week. I will have my siblings and Mike at nighttime.

We will not walk alone. We need to keep our faith and stay positive as we take baby steps. Mom was so still tonight.

I feel this week I can really finally say I love my Mom enough to let her go. When we were in Mom's room, we gathered around Mom's bed. Darcy said, "We should say the Lord's Prayer together." Mom started the prayer. I could feel the warmth in the room as we all prayed with Mom. Time for another group hug. Then Mom slept.We all got to laughing tonight about dumb things. Laughter has been our best medicine. I feel it has helped us all stay strong and helped us ease things when we are all so powerless.

Tuesday, March 8, 2005

Dear God — I feel my faith is slipping at times. I feel so powerless. It is hard to sit back when one feels so powerless. I know I have to let go, let God. I'm getting tired, and I want to stay strong to keep Mom in her home. If it is meant to be, it will be. I know she is getting worse as I sit next to her each day. Mom and her family need one of your angels by our sides. They have been to see Mom. She has been talking to them at night. I pray for us all.

This is starting to break my heart. Mom is lying so still. I have lived with no regrets during this journey. I'm so happy for that. We have had a good family life. Mom and Dad worked hard when we were young; they did their best. We all have lots of memories to share, then getting

Mom's cancer news, all coming together, we did nothing but laugh, joke and eat and be happy the last few months. We have not had really sad days, only the last few. I live with no regrets. I will be the happiest person when Mom leaves this world since the last few weeks she has suffered so. It kills me when she looks up at me and asks, "What's wrong with me?" I just tell her the truth, that she will not die alone. We all have held her hands so tight.

This morning when Mom woke up, she tried to get the phlegm out of her mouth, but it would not come out. We tried putting her on her side but that did not help. It is a powerless feeling to stand there. I just have to ask God to help her. We will be her protectors and do what we can until our job is done. Finally Mom could rest.

We are taking turns having naps. The volunteers will start again tomorrow. Then Chuck, Bruce, Darcy, Mike and I will do the nights as planned. This is about teamwork. Mom taught us this in the restarant business, and now we are using it in this cancer journey. We had a quiet night.

Wednesday, March 9, 2005

Dear God – Today is a new day. We need to face each day with open arms. We know Mom is suffering. When it is time, we will accept it as a gift from You. We are all doing our best to take care of Mom. Please help our angel, Marvel Mae

My midnight shift has started. It feels so different. I can not explain it. Mom is making funny noices. I can hear the death rattle. The house is so quiet. The air feels so heavy; I can't explain this feeling. I need to keep myself busy, so I write my thoughts into a poem. I pray Mom will be an angel soon.

Mom/Friend
What do you do when you're so powerless?
All I can think of is pray.
I hear your lungs filling up
And listen to the death rattle.
You have been starting to turn purple
And sinking within.
I want to stay so strong.
But I am so scared.

Living for the Moment

I want to hear your voice once again.
Buck up! And take it, and don't be a wimp.
It is so hard to hear you slipping away.
The time is coming, and I know it will be okay.
You have suffered so.
And it is time for it to end.
I will stay strong.
As it was ordered by you.
But you have always been a friend.
I keep thinking one more rattle and this will all end.
I light a candle to let it burn
In hoping God will see
And come and get my friend.
I hope today is the day.
Sunday was your day as you wished,
But we will take whatever comes. So please go in peace, as your
dream may come true today.

Yesterday morning Darcy told Jade and Megan to pray to Jesus that he will take Grandma Marvel to Him. This morning Darcy asked the girls if they had prayed.

"Yes, I did," replied Jade.

"I did during math class because that teacher is so boring," Megan explained.

Mom would have loved to hear that. I may have to tell her that later today. My shift this morning is a long one. I can not explain it in words. It is like the air is so heavy. Once in awhile, I step out on the deck for some fresh air. I have been thinking of Mom's funeral. She planned it all—the music that we have played over and over, the reading, the flowers, and the menu (we will serve BBQ pork sandwiches with her secert BBQ sauce receipe). She planned her final send off herself. It was a final gathering, and she wanted everyone to smile and remember the good times. I will be patient and not take a moment for granted.

Mom gave me her mother's pincushion. She told me when she died to hold onto this tight as she was going to be with her mother soon. One does a lot of thinking in the middle of the night like this.

139

Brenda Ann Rebelein

When Chuck woke up at 6:00 am, he went into Mom's bedroom for a few minutes. This is something he never does. He ususally just goes out the door after we talk a few minutes about what kind of night she had. I feel Chuck had his final goodbye. Mike and I told him we would call if something different happens. I think Chuck knew then what was going to happen. Bruce called to see how the night went. We would keep him posted.We checked on Mom. Mike looked at me and told me, "Brenda, I think we're close to losing her." I had a sigh of relief. Darcy stopped in to see how things were going. I told her things were different. Last night it was hard to explain the noises Mom was making and how her breathing was so different. Mom made me promise to take care of Darcy. She is the baby. Mike told Darcy this morning in Mom's bedroom that he would be canceling our reservation today for the rooms at the casino for Mom's birthday. We could not go now. Darcy and I agreed they had to be canceled. We remembered Mom saying, "On no certain terms do you cancel your reservations."

It was medication time. Mike, Darcy and I decided we still should give Mom her medications since Darcy was there to help us. Then at least she would pain free to heaven if it was her time. So Darcy helped Mike and me one last final time.

Mom was lying there so still. She was looking so peaceful. Darcy did not know if she wanted to go to work or not. It was payroll time, and that is something you can not really put off. She only needed one hour to work, then she could stop back. Mike and I told her to go and we would call her the minute things changed. Darcy went out the door. Mike called a friend of ours who is a nurse. She told Mike that we were only minutes away from Mom passing away. As God is my witness, I feel He waited until Darcy left so He could spare her the pain when Mom took her final breath. Mom wanted to protect Darcy one more time. It all happened so fast. I was in the other bedroom. Mike said, "Brenda you better grab your pincushion. I think the time is now."

I could not think. I was running around the bedroom looking for my grandma's pincushion to hold. I finally found it. I ran to Mom's bedside as she left this world. She gurgled a couple of times and took a few deep breaths, then it was over. She looked so peaceful when she went to go to a better place called home. Mike called Darcy to turn her car around and come back, he called Bruce and Chuck to come home.

140

Living for the Moment

They had to get Chuck's boss to come and take over the trucking load that Chuck was hauling. I think Mike was trying to protect me at this time. I had seen the good days and the bad. I would not live with regrets now.

We were living for the moment. Darcy came back home. Bruce and Wendy came, and Thelma came from work. Darcy called Jeremy.

At 8:45 this morning, Mom made peace. Someone called hospice and Pastor Soli.

Dear God – Thank you, thank you, for taking our angel, Marvel Mae. She is now pain-free. She can now take care of us from up above. I pray for Mom's safe journey. God rest Mom's soul. Help this family as we come to the close of our cancer journey. We will go in peace. Hear my prayer of thanks, God.

Hospice came in full force. There was the nurse and the social worker, our earth angel who answered all our cries for help on those bad days. I remember how they just took over the situation. They went in Mom's room alone. They removed all the medication from the house or dumped it in a garbage bag for disposal. They called the funeral home for us. All we did was grieve our loss. I asked Mike to call Monica, Lance, and Kristine. Jeanette was going to pick up Josh at the high school and bring him to our house. They would wait there until we got home. Monica was next door at Sheila's. My biggest blessing is the way Mike helped me so much. I just had to take care of me. They had to go and get the grandchildren out of school, so they would not hear about Grandma passing away from someone else. Chuck finally got home to us. They would do nothing until Chuck got back home.

Pastor Soli and Marvel's children and spouses went in to bless her life and her new place we call home. Everyone took turns going in there and saying their final goodbyes. I was walking around in a fog. My job was done. I did not know what to do as I walked around aimlessly. Darcy came to me. "Brenda, you need to say goodbye to Mom. Have your time alone with her." I did as I was told. I went in Mom's bedroom and closed the door. I still saw her as my patient. I looked around at the final medications that needed to be disposed of and threw them in a bag. The whole time, I was talking to Mom aloud, to my patient, Marvel Mae, telling her how honored I was to take care of her. My job

141

was done. "Thanks for staying so postive and strong; it made my job easier." I prayed for her safe trip. When I turned around and looked at her, she became my mom only, no more a patient. Then I sat next to Mom in her bed and I said, "Goodbye to the best mom I could have ever been blessed with. I love you, Mom. Until we meet again, God bless you, my angel, my mom." I kissed her one more final time.

The funeral home where Mom was taken is owned by our clients. Who are also friends. The two funeral directors that came and got Mom are two good friends of ours. We worked side by side each week until I started staying at Mom's full time. Having them come and get Mom made it all the more special. I could tell it was hard on them too. They had been waiting for this call. Their smiles and hugs were so welcomed. They gave us all the time we needed to say goodbye. When they removed Mom, I told them to take care of her. She was a very special lady. They promised me they would. Mom was going to be cremated.

One can not say enough for hospice in a time like this When we called hospice and told them Mom had cancer, they took over and helped us. They guided us through this journey. Our social worker was a call away. Our nurses answered all our questions no matter how dumb they were. Our bath lady was our friend and helped us keep Mom clean and bed sore free. All the people in the office who answered our cries of help. This is a bond you can not find any where else.

When it was time for Mom to leave this world, we called them, and they took over once again. They made our wish come true. Mom never had to leave her home. I will never forget my hospice experience. Some day Darcy and I hope to help someone as they helped us.

When everyone left, it was Chuck, Thelma, Mike and I. Chuck and I sat down and had a waffle together in Mom's memory with extra butter and syrup. It was a good memory we all shared. I grabbed all the clothes and items I had brought to stay at Mom's. We laughed as I had almost as much stuff here as Mom did. Let's just say I filled the pickup with my things. I grabbed my angel that helped us through our cancer journey. The last few weeks were tough. That will go away soon. I will not think of the bad. Mom is right. It is good to think of the good times. We had a good time, we laughed and played jokes. I will live with no regrets as my life will move on without my mom.

Living for the Moment

The first poem I read to Mom when she passed away. The second poem I read after she had passed away, when the family and Pastor Soli gathered around to bless her life.

Mom: Marvel Mae Bartelt Niebuhr

You saw me take my first breath,
And now I watch you take your last.
It breaks my heart and makes me feel sad,
And the tears will fall.
As God is my witness, you've given me a good life
since I took my first breath.
I pray for your safe journey,
As we see you slip away.
Tell Dad I love him.
When you walk through the gates,
Keep that strong smile I love to see.
I will wait for a yellow butterfly breathing close to me,
Knowing that is you saying you'll always be near me!

Dear God

Our work is done.
You have given us the tools to keep her in her own home, as this was her wish.
Thank you for guiding us each day,
And for hearing my prayers.
You carried me when I needed it the most.
Take care of Mom as You are getting the best.
Thanks for the many years.
It is time for her to go home now, and we will understand.
Mom has gone in peace.
God, hear my prayer. Amen.

Brenda Ann Rebelein

Thursday, March 10, 2005

Dear God – Thank you for taking our mom, grandma, and friend to make her our angel from above. We all have so many memories of her. That is what she wants us to do: talk about them, laugh, and share a joke. Always follow your dreams and have faith, be strong. Thank you for setting us all free. I'm grateful you never gave up on me. The days I was scared I was losing my faith, you only carried me higher. Hear my prayer of thanks.

Today was my first day without Mom. I can not help but feel sad and lonely. I know Mom would be smiling down at me, saying,"Buck up and don't be a wimp." We were all told that many times when she had to straighten us out. I'm sick to my stomach. I can smell the death smell on my clothes. I will get the washing machine going. It is so weird being home. I catch myself looking at the clock, thinking of medication time, or wondering if the nurse and bath lady come today. *Should call and see how Mom's day is going? Talk to the caretaker on duty?* Last night when we got home I could not sleep. I kept waking up thinking about the medication time and who's shift it was now. I knew I had to face it, now it is over. Our prayers have been answered, Mom suffers no more. My siblings have been calling to talk. I want to hide from the world.

We go to the funeral home at 2:00 today to make the arrangements for Mom's funeral. She has it so planned out that this should be easy for us. That is the way she wanted it, and she did not want us to mess it up. It was the last party she would give. Pastor Soli met us there. We shared stories and had a few laughs. It makes it easlier to keep it light just like Mom wanted. Mom will get the service she wanted, the L-shaped flowers with a candle in the middle and 42 carnations, one for every member of the family, the BBQ Pork sandwiches with her secert BBQ sauce, salads and chocolate cake with pickles on the side. The sandwiches will be made by Darcy and Jeremy at the Meat Market.

Mom is going to be cremated. That will take a few days.We are having a private family meeting at the church to remember the good times with Mom before the cancer on Sunday night, the night we were to come home from Mom's birthday party. Then Monday night is visitation at the funeral home. On Tuesday is Mom's funeral. This weekend is her birthday party at the casino. We had to decide to stay home or go anyway. We all knew what Mom would have wanted.

Living for the Moment

Under no terms should we stay home. In her memory, we are going in the morning. She would be happy we are following through with her plans. It was weird being Mike was canceling our rooms, and not much longer after, Mom passes away. That is her way of telling us to go. I miss you, Mom.

Friday, March 11, 2005

Dear God – Help us all have a safe trip to the casino. I know Mom is proud we are fulfilling her wish to go to her birthday party without her. I will be strong, I will be okay. I'm so grateful Mom is at peace with you.

Mike, Josh and I left for the casnio at 8:00 this morning. Mom always rode with us and hollered at Mike's driving all the way. She made a good backseat driver. She was always sitting on her deck with her small suitcase, jiggling the coins in her coat pocket, when we got there to pick her up. It is hard holding back the tears. I miss her so much. I have so many mixed feelings about this trip. Mike and Josh know me too well. They knew what I was thinking. They helped me and explained why we had to go as planned. How happy Mom would be if she knew we were following through with another one of her wishes. We need to enjoy this day. She would have been upset if I had stayed home to cry.

We stopped at Mom's favorite place to eat. We stop here every year. I had Mom's french toast and burnt bacon in her memory. Hot tea to warm the soul. This trip is bringing back so many fun memories. We have laughed all morning. Mom and I planned some of this trip. We both knew she was not going to make the trip. She still wanted to have some laughs. I brought her winter coat with me. It is black with white spots, and I brought her butterfly purse. I did not tell Mike and Josh. We stopped at the grocery store, and the wind was blowing so hard I grabbed Mom's coat and purse and jumped out of the pickup. Mike and Josh looked at me. It was so funny. I was laughing so hard. I told them Mom told me to wear it, have fun with it. We were walking into the store, and I was laughing so hard. They were making fun of me. They thought I looked 40 years older then I am. They did not want to walk with me. I was talking to them, and they did not follow me. When I came in the store there was a lady giving out food samples. I was still

145

Brenda Ann Rebelein

laughing, and she was laughing with me though she did not know why I was laughing. She had a good laugh with me. They did not come in the store with me. So there I stood, laughing with Mom's coat and purse all by myself. Finally, they came in shaking their heads. I wanted to buy a cake. They tried to tell me that you do not buy a birthday cake for someone who has died. Next year, Mom, you will have a birthday cake. I got some waffles for breakfast. We get the hospitality room with a little kitchenette and sitting room with a large table so we can all bring food and have a place to go to visit.

On Mom's last birthday, we had a blast. We always go early to play the machines before everyone gets there. Mom was screamimg and clapping her hands. I tried to get her to calm down because she had only won $3.00. There was a group of young guys circled around her, looking how much she had one. They looked blankly at this strange woman who had only won $3.00 She winked at me. It had been a boring afternoon. She wanted to liven it up. What a better way than to have a group of young guys circling around her. That woman never surprised us. She would see one of us coming, and she would leave the machine with some credits on so we could have some fun and finish out the credits. Mom always wanted to have fun no matter where she was.

It was scary going in the casnio without Mom. I knew I had to stand up tall and have a good time. I do not gamble much because I think I work too hard for my money. I usually helped Mom get change, sat by her machine so she could use the bathroom, cashed money for her, and talked with her. She would have someone to shake, someone to hit if she lost. It was fun watching her. Then I would go for awhile and come back to check on her. I looked around. The old feelings of looking for Mom are coming back when I go to her favorite spot. Now it is only strangers.

I will stay out of the casnio. That is not a place for me. It is too early for me, missing Mom so much. The kids are watching a movie and eating pizza. I need to be with my family. We will help each other in our time of need. When I go back to our room, Little Blake was singing "Happy Birthday, Grandma Marvel." Someone asked him why he was doing that. "Well, it's her birthday party, isn't it? She told us to be happy." The kids wanted to know where the birthday cake was? The

Living for the Moment

adults thought I was losing it, but the kids understand. Next year, kids, we will have one. Look, Mom, no tears.

Saturday, March 12, 2005

Dear God – Help me stay strong this weekend. I know I will be okay. I will keep the lunch going and make sure everyone gets fed. Thank you for the healthy food you have given us. I cherish that we can follow through on Mom's birthday wish. She is with us in heart and soul. Bless this day.

The last two days we have had fun. We have laughed and shared some jokes. Every once in awhile someone will want to talk about Grandma. This has been good therapy for our family. Once in awhile, I bring Mom's coat and butterfly purse out and head for the casnio. Then I take her picture and rub it on a machine for luck. I do it to change the mood. It keeps everything light and fun. Guess what, I'm just going home with a bent up picture. This was our first test living without Mom. It came so soon. We all did our best to have a good time. We all knew what was on everyone's minds. It was good to get home. Sunday at 7:00 p.m., we are going to the church for a family meeting. We will be talking about Mom, Grandma and friend. What will we miss the most? What did we like about her? It was hard for people to talk in front of everyone. We all deal with grief in different ways. We will all miss different things about her. For me it is the phone calls. How many times did I get grounded for going over my calls? The kids use to get grounded, so Mom did too. They had fun with that one. I will go to the cemetary and talk things out with Mom. What I liked the most about my mom was her outgoing personality, positive attitiude, her non judgmental style and her good advice when your answer was always right in front of you all along. It has been a long weekend. And a nice closing of Mom's birthday celebration with a get together with family to talk about our favorite person, Marvel Mae.

Monday, March 14, 2005

Dear God – Please watch over our family. Today is Mom's visitation at the funeral home. It is a good day to talk about the good times to, to share a story and put a smile on someone's face when we talk about "remember when." I'm glad Mom's suffering is over. I will accept where my life is going. Bless Mom's life.

147

Wow … We had so many people at the funeral home. Mom was in the restaurant business for twenty years, so she met a lot of people. She was shining down on us the whole night. She was seeing who was there, and she was happy for each person that had crossed her path during her life. They were thinking about 400 hundred people were there. The four of us kids were up greeting our vistors. It was all so pretty up front. There was Mom's picture, her flowers with her candle and 42 carnations, one for each of us, the favorite poems some of us made for her, then her urn. She received 35 flowers in her memory. The family brought us sips of water. There was a steady stream of people. We could not leave the line. We laughed because there were people that we did not know who came. There were shirt-tail relatives or people who Mom worked with years ago. They thought I was married to Chuck. It made my night as I teased him. Mom would have been proud. It went as she planned. This is part of her send off.

Tuesday, March 15, 2005

Dear God – Today is Mom's funeral. You sent us a beautiful, sunny day as you open the doors to heaven. Did Mom order this? Please give me the courage I need to read my poem at the funeral. Mom told me she would give me the strength I need. Watch over all of our family and friends as we gather together to celebrate Mom's life. Our memories will keep us warm as we build more together.

We were gifted to have a perfect day. God and Mom sent this to us. We had to laugh. We hope Mom is not trying to take control up there in heaven. Mom even planned her forecast. When we went to the church, we were gathered outside for a few minutes. When we went to go inside, a flock of geese flew over the church. I feel it was sign from God that Mom is okay, those geese she watched every day until the end.

Mom had a big funeral. So many friends and family gathered to celebrate her life. It made the day so special when I saw the hospice staff and volunteers with their smiles and warm hugs. The nurses helped us so much, I can not express in enough words what they mean to us. They helped us keep Mom in her home and taught us how to take care of her medically, emotionally and physically. We learned how to build a support team to take care of our loved one. I will always remember the family and friends who helped us.

Living for the Moment

A few minutes before the funeral, I saw a friend who lost her husband a few years ago. He was a good customers of Mom's when she was in business. She gave me a gift in his memory. She thought he would want me to have this. I wanted to find a corner and cry. I took that glass cross with me with a prayer on it that said part of Mom's heart will always be with me. I said a small quick prayer to God, Mom, and the friend I had lost to help me. It went with me when I had to get up in front of everyone to read my poem. I did just fine, I did it for me. It was a promise I made to Mom and myself on one of those nights when we could just sit and talk.

Pastor Soli talked about Mom not being afraid of dying, but she was afraid of mice. He talked about how he would come to visit Mom and she would help him with her words of encouragement. He talked about how she loved her family and friends and the way she cooked for people, even the ones she did not know. Mom's music was beautiful. Just like we heard on the good and the bad days. Our singer had such a strong voice. It had to be hard for her to sing for her friend. She did an outstanding job. Mom planned a very nice service. The cemetery is always a hard one for me. I will be spending a lot of time here. It is my place to feel comfort. Mom's lunch was good. Everyone enjoyed Mom's BBQ sauce once again. Darcy and Jeremy supplied the pork.

After the funeral, we took the leftover food and went to Mom's to do thank you cards right away. I wanted to go home and rest, but Darcy was right. There were so many people there, we needed to get started so we could get our lives back together again. There were a few of us there. I was about to do something I should not have done. It is an inside joke. I wanted to break the ice and make everyone laugh. It was like Mom was there. I had a cough syrup bottle in my hand and the lid flew off. There was cough syrup everywhere, all over my good clothes, the table, the carpet, the wall. We laughed so hard, and we all thought of Mom right away because she would be telling me to behave. I had taken all my clothes home. I needed something to wear. She had her pajamas and robes in her closet. Then I found the blue dress we have laughed about. She wore it to every wedding and every funeral. Do I take the chance and wear this for a joke? I took the chance. I came around the corner walking like Mom. "Hello guys, Marvel returns." By then everyone was there. The blue dress strikes again. We all laughed as everyone said I have the same shape as Mom. We did 500 thank you's, and when we get home, there will be more waiting in the mailboxes. We all had a job to do, so it went fast. We had supper and called it a day. I received three house plants and three mum plants from the funeral. The mum plants are going in my memory rock garden. I have a flower to represent each loved one I lost in my life. I can enjoy them each year. I love my family. Each one of them means something to me in their own special way. I'm the lucky one to have them in my life.

Wednesday, March 16, 2005

Dear God — I hope you and Mom are enjoying your day. I'm so happy for her. She has nothing but happiness ahead of her. We know she has a good time no matter where she is at. I send Happy Birthday wishes her way.

Today is Mom's birthday. I have tried to stay busy. She is in a good place with no pain. My life is starting to settle down, and I'm working with Mike. I'm happy I can live with no regrets. Mom and I had a good time. I think of the time we all had together, and it puts a smile on my face. I did some more thank you's, and we ended up sending out 600 cards. Mom had touched a lot of lives. The family called each other to see how everyone was doing. We were all thinking of Mom today. Today was a blessing for her. I'm so glad we followed through and went to the casino as Mom wanted. Things have all fallen into place like they should. Happy Birthday, Mom.

Thursday, March 17, 2005

Dear God — I miss Mom so much today. It is hard now that things have settled down and gone back to their normal life. I know she is watching over us every day. I need to be grateful her cancer journey is over. I know she is in a good place. She is with you, God.

I have been working with Mike, doing what I can. I have now come down with a sinus infection. I came down with it the day after the funeral. My body is telling me enough of this, it is time to rest. I will not be selfish and wish Mom was here. I reread my poems about her pain and wanting this all to end. Then I think about the fun time we had together, so why feel bad? My emotions go up and down some days. I can not sleep at night. They say that is normal. The night of the funeral, I dreamt Mom was trying to talk to me. She wanted to tell me something. I remember screaming at her. "You died. Leave me alone. My work is done. What do you want from me?" I tossed and turned all night. When I woke up, I had stripped all the bedding off the bed. I could still feel the struggle in the morning. I wish I could open my arms to her. I was fighting something that could have been so beautiful. I pray she comes back to see me. She told me she would send me a sign when she gets to heaven safely.

Saturday, March 19, 2005

Dear God – We know that Mom is safe with you. We received the twenty inches of snow today. I knew she would send a sign, but Mom has always been one to do it up right. Thanks, God and Mom, for the snow.

This morning we started the snow removal with the businesses at 3:00 am. We were all talking about Grandma. She told me she was going to die in the spring, and I would go right into spring cleanup, and she would send me work so I would not have the time to rest from taking care of her. I would go right to work. "I will send you a message when I get to heaven." Mike had to go back home. The snow blower was not working. It is March, so the snow is wet and heavy, and when we get twenty inches, it is even worse. Josh and I were uptown trying to shovel the wet snow. Josh looks up in the sky, saying, "Okay, Grandma, no more snow. We know that you're in heaven." Josh's voice just echoed through the street. We both had to laugh knowing she sent us the work for the day. Thinking of her made us smile as we saw her final send off in twenty inches of snow.

We all have new beginnings now that our cancer journey has come to the end. Mom is safe and looking down from up above. I will cherish each day when I wake up knowing that this is a gift from God. It is my choice what kind of day that I want to have.

Friday, March 24, 2005

Dear God – Today is my birthday. This is the special day you picked for me. I will receive this gift with open arms. I will spend it with my family and keep things simple. Thank you God for this gifted day.

Brenda Ann Rebelein

Sunday, March 27 [Easter Day]

Dear God – Help us all through the day today. This is our first holiday without Mom. I have been counting my blessings each day. I have been working on my grief in my own way and thinking of you and Mom on this day.

Today I think of all the holidays Mom and I worked side by side in the restaurant business. Those were some fun years. It was always a big challenge for me to get those tables set up right the first time. I would hear a holler knowing we'd redo this one more time. We always put on an awesome feast with a smorgasbord on holidays and Sundays. We relished the joy on the customers' faces when we saw another satisfied person leave her restaurant. Now Mom is smiling down from her restaurant in the sky.

We went to Chuck and Thelma's for Easter Dinner today. It was fun watching the kids hunt for their Easter eggs, thinking of the fun Mom always had hiding the eggs from the kids by her house and her deck by the lake. Happy Easter, Mom. God Bless our memories.

Chapter 7

Final Wishes and the Closing of Our Journey

Mom has been gone now for two months. I'm so grateful to hospice for sending me pamphlets to help me with baby steps as I walk through life without my mom. The feelings I have had are all normal. That is a good feeling, to know I do not have to be alone. They are helping me to learn where I go from here. They have grief sessions I can go to, but right now I feel I'm doing okay. I will still keep a journal because I have always loved to write. I may have to start a new one about my life.

Tuesday, May 3, 2005

Dear God – I'm doing okay. I have been trying to stay busy with my new life without Mom. She is my guardian angel now. She has helped me out a lot already. I know you work through people. Hospice is having a speaker tonight to talk about her cancer story, about her mother and the book she wrote. Thank you for sending her to me. I'm so grateful to hospice for helping me grieve.

Darcy and I are going to the grief class together tonight. I will keep an open mind as I walk through the doors. Where do I go from here? They will teach me that I will not be alone. In a couple of weeks, we will be cleaning out Mom's house so Monica can move in. I will need strength as we pass out Mom's personal things. We are so lucky Mom would not settle down until she had the most important things handed out herself. Most of the hard work is done. We have decided it will be just us four kids. When we go through Mom's things, we will leave as adults, after starting there as babies. This has brought us all so close as a family. We are all thinking of each other.

Monica will be moving into Grandma's house. Mom's wish will be coming true. I remember the visits I had with Mom as she laid in bed. How she prayed this would happen. Everything is so final. It can be scary at times. That is why tonight I will go and listen.

153

Brenda Ann Rebelein

Darcy and I went out for supper. Then we went to the meeting. When we walked into the room, I could feel the love. The hospice staff, volunteers, and people who had lost loved ones and had hospice in their homes. The hugs we received when I came through the door will always be remembered. We saw our nurses, the bath lady, and the volunteers that were at Mom's house the last week. One could feel the warmth in the room.

Cynthia Watts was the speaker from Sioux Falls, SD. She wrote the book, *God's Ribbons*. She told us her story about her mom's cancer story, and she wrote a book of poems named messages of hope. Her story was so close to ours. Darcy and I kept looking at each other. You are sure she is not talking about our mom? The humor she had until the end, the way she lived before cancer, how she was not sick the whole journey until the end, how she never complained. She always kept a positive attitude. It sounded just like just our mom. Her mom did not want help until the end when she had to have it. Her mom also talked to the angels before she left to heaven, just like Mom. Their stories were so much the same. Darcy and I were listening to every word with great content.

Cynthia talked about how her writing had become her book, and how the thoughts would come out of nowhere. She would write on any scrap piece of paper. I could relate so much to what she was saying about her writing and the loss of a mom. I felt her speech from the heart. Mom and I had talked about my writing. I remember one night, while sitting next to Mom's bed in the middle of night, she looked at me. "Won't it be something if we could help one person with your writing? Oh, I sure hope so." I squeezed her hand. Mom stood behind me and gave me the faith I needed. That was a big reason I kept the journal. I knew I needed a place to write. I can always remember her courage and strength. She taught me to go forward and follow my dreams. As Cynthia was speaking, I could see myself talking about Mom and keeping her alive and spreading the word that a cancer journey can be an unforgettable experience. It does not have to be a bad time. Cancer can take our loved ones, but we will always have the love and memories that last a lifetime. We should enjoy the time we have left with our loved ones. Make the good times outlast the bad; they are only moments.

Living for the Moment

Darcy and I got to visit with her afterwards. It was like she was telling our story. She gave me hope that maybe I should follow through with my writing. I was too excited to sleep when I got home. That is nothing new. I do not sleep at night, and this is part of my dealing with grief. It was a very overwhelming night for Darcy and me. In the middle of the night, I kept thinking of making my dream of a book become a reality. I know God will help me through this journey, as I cross over another part of my life. God will give me the guidance, faith, and courage to honor my mom.

I miss Mom so much tonight. I listen to her funeral music. There's something about it that makes me stronger. My tears soon dry up, and I'm grateful for the time we had. It puts a smile on my face, thinking about what she would be up to next. It reminds me of our time together. I listen to the music over and over. It helps takes the pain away, knowing I live with no regrets.

Sunday, May 8, 2005 [Mother's Day]

Dear God – Today was a tough one for me. It is our first Mother's Day without Mom. I talked with my siblings as we were checking on each other to see how the day was going. I cannot stop thinking about her even though I know we have her arms wrapped around us. Thank you for giving us the best mother of all. Today she is with her mother. I pray they are having a good day together. I know Mom was looking forward to being with her again. I wish them a good day from someone who loves them so.

A person I know from hospice called to wish me a Happy Mother's Day. She was thinking of me since this was my first Mother's Day without Mom. This made my day knowing someone was thinking and praying for me. There are so many good people out there. Once again I feel the warmth of hospice. Today, I feel, was the first day I felt the grief of losing Mom. I think about how she prepared us for her death. We learned how to be strong, focused on the good things in life, and how to make the best out of the life she had been given.

We went out for dinner, and then we came home. I went to the cemetery alone to be with Mom. This is our time just like we had before. I had a good cry; this was so long overdue. I asked Mom to help me give me the strength to go on. I finally dealt with my pain as

Brenda Ann Rebelein

I crumbled on Mom's grave. I asked her if she thought I was doing okay. I told her I wanted a sign from her to know if I was doing okay. I know she is safe in heaven since she sent twenty inches of snow. I wanted to know how she was doing in the better place called heaven with no pain.

I went home. It was really getting dark out fast. A storm had popped up out of nowhere. We could see some rain coming, after being home for 45 minutes. The wind and rain came up with large gusts. We had hail also hitting the house. You can call me nuts, but this scared me. This storm came up too fast for me. Josh has a fear of storms, and Grandma has been helping him face his fears. I told Mike and Josh that I had gone to go see Grandma and shared with them what I had talked about. Josh looked outside at the storm and then turned to me. "Mom, you are not allowed to go and see Grandma alone any more. We will go with you." I had to laugh knowing Mom was getting the last word once again. Is she controlling my grief process too? You would have to know my Mom to understand. She wanted no grief, only happiness.

I was thinking back when we would call Mom to wish her a Happy Mother's Day. She would giggle and say, "You are too late. One of the siblings already called." We all wanted to be the first one. Then we found out she was teasing us. Who really knows who the first one was. She would sit back and chuckle. I miss Mom's humor. She always had fun no matter where she went. I hope to make her proud. I know one thing, there was never a doubt how much she loved her family. She was the rock of our family. We all knew how to make her proud and be the best we can be.

Sunday, May 15, 2005 [Cleaning out Mom's house]

Dear God – I have been doing well. My prayers to start each day out have helped. I need to be strong today as we go through Mom's things at the house. It is a new beginning and a way of putting closure to the past. I will keep the faith while I know you will walk me through the day.

Chuck, Bruce, Darcy, and I are going to clean Mom's house out today. We decided if you want it, you buy it, and then we will keep that money going in Mom's account for expenses. Monica is going to rent the house for a year to see if this is something she wants for herself

156

Living for the Moment

and the girls. Paul [Sheila's husband] helped us put things in our piles as we bought each item. Thelma was making us supper.

We had a good day together. We laughed when we remembered something from our past or found certain things that made us smile. Halfway through the day I gave Chuck, Bruce and Darcy their gag gifts from Mom. This was another one of Mom's wishes she had put together the night we cleaned out her closet in her bedroom. Mom always wanted the last laugh. They were things that made Mom laugh. She wanted to make this day easier for us. Everything went well today. When we went through the china cabinet, it was hard for me. I had to go to the bathroom to be alone for a few minutes. Some things had memories, and a lot of it we had never seen before. There was a baking dish that Darcy, Jeremy and the girls gave Mom for Christmas one year. Mom had packed it away. We all laughed. This was the dish Mom thought one of us had taken home. She thought we had taken food home and never brought it back, and here she had never used it. We made Darcy buy it back for $2.00. We gave Bruce all the deck of cards we found. Bruce and Mom loved playing solitaire. We had a whole day of things like this to help us through. Maybe it was right, maybe it was wrong, the way we did things, but us together, the children of Marvel, made it a special day for me, being alone with my siblings and being selfish just for today. There were a lot of memories here to go through in one day. I just wanted it done, so I could go on with my life. We did the whole house in one day. It helped that Lance and Kristine had cleaned the basement before this cancer journey started, even though we think Mom knew then that something was wrong with her. Things happen for a reason. Mom had gotten rid of a lot of things herself, so there was less for us to do. Today we received the things we knew we were receiving from Mom. Yes, I received the ugly pictures on the wall that Mom willed to me. She loved them so much. I had tried getting her to replace them for so many years. She even told Mike what wall she wanted them on at my house. She wanted them right above the couch. She laughed telling Mike this as she was giving her last orders for when she was gone.

When we were sorting through the basement, all the memories came flooding back to us. This is where we all slept, had fun, and where we had fights as siblings. We talked about our childhood and how we

Brenda Ann Rebelein

lived in this little house. It was a nice place to call home. I got many treasures that day to remember Mom by, things that bring a smile to my face when I look at them. She would be so happy things went so well. We all were happy as we closed the door on our past.

Monday, May 16, 2005

Dear God – I know change is good. We need to improve on Mom's house before Monica can move in. We are cleaning and painting today to give the house a fresh start. You gave us the tools to receive. I felt her smiling down at us today as we worked, trying to make her final wishes come true.

Mike did most of the painting, and I did some painting, but mostly I did the taping. Monica, Lance and Kristine came and finished up the last of the painting. We hired someone to come in and do the ceilings. They have the old-fashioned speckle look. It looked so nice when it was done. I do wish Mom was here to enjoy this, but she is smiling from above. She would want Monica to enjoy this. She told her that in the bedroom that day when she finally talked again after being silent so long. The house looks good, Mom.

Sunday, May 22, 2005 [Finally finish cleaning out the house]

Dear God – I'm taking one day at a time. Things are getting easier with time and healing for me. It is good getting my life back to normal. When the pain gets overwhelming, on the rough days, I grab my journal or poems. I know I had to love my patient/mom enough to let her go. Time moves on, and each day is a blessing and a gift. It is my choice as to what I will do with it.

God, I may need some extra strength today as we take out the final personal things of our mom and dad out of the house they built as a couple to start a family. Monica will start another generation in the house, and, who know who will get it next as we move on in years. Today we close the past and start our future.

Today was a day with so many emotions. I feel good about where we are all headed. Life goes on, and we all need to face changes. We are closing the doors on our childhood one final time. Mom will always be a woman I admire. There are so many emotions one goes through at a time like this. God needed our angel, Marvel Mae. We did a good job

Living for the Moment

taking care of Mom just as she took care of us all those years. We can take all the memories with us as we close the door one final time.

Saturday, May 28, 2005 [Monica, Desiree and Destiny move in]

Dear God — You gave us a beautiful day for Monica and the girls to move into Grandma's house. Mom's wishes did come true. I can see Mom smiling down on the house today, liking the new look. The geese are here to complete the day by talking the day away to each other. I will keep an open mind. Today is about acceptance.

Chuck, Thelma, Mike, Josh and I are camping together for the weekend at Mom's favorite place to camp. This is where my camper sits during camping season. We decided to check out the movers. We made a hot dish for them to eat when they needed a break. Monica had Sheila, Paul, Courtney, Tony, Blake and some friends help her move in.

When I stepped in for the first time, all the boxes were sitting around, and the furniture was waiting to find its place. I had to step back outside for a minute. It was like it took my breath away for a minute. I could feel Mom's arms around me as I stepped into Monica's house for the first time. I was thinking about all the talks Mom and I had about making this happen.

A few years ago, I gave Monica a set of china. I told her I would keep them safe in my china cabinet until she had her own home. She had been living in apartments since she started raising a family. This morning, I went to her new home, put the china in her china cabinet, and left a note: Welcome home, Monica. I'm new in the house. I need a place to live. I'm right where I belong. I'm something you have waited for years to have. What am I? I left the note on a chair by the door, and a few hours later she read it and called me. She knew right away what it was. The china she had wanted for years now had a place in a home of her own. It looked nice in Grandma's china cabinet which fills the wall.

It warmed my heart knowing that Mom's wish was happening, but we still had her final wish to come true. The day of Mom died, Monica met up with a high school friend named Chad. They are now dating. We will see where things go from here. Things do happen for a reason. Monica says Grandma sent him to her that day, and they have been together ever since.

159

Brenda Ann Rebelein

Monica is so happy today, and the girls are glowing as they run from room to room. They love their new backyard. They are dancing on their new deck that looks over the lake. They now have lots of room to run and grow. Mom's house will be filled up with fun, games and laughter. That was what Mom was all about. God bless this house, and may new memories be built.

Saturday, June 11, 2005 [Hospice Fundraiser Walk]

Dear God — We are blessed with another nice day today. The hospice walk is a five-mile walk in memory of a loved one who had hospice or who are staff or volunteers. We are walking in memory of Mom and Grandma. Please watch over us walkers. I pray for our safety. Thank you, God, for the day you have given us. We all walk together to help this fundraiser.

The meeting place was the county fairgrounds. It was a five-mile walk around part of the local lake. They had hospice T-shirts, ice water and treats for us and always met us with a smile and a warm hug. To me hospice gave a new meaning for the word compassion when we went on our cancer journey. Chuck, Sheila, Paul, Courtney, Blake, Monica, Jade and I went on the hospice walk. Monica and Sheila made us T-shirts with Mom's picture on it and the words "Marvel Mae Niebuhr – Our mom, grandma and friend (with yellow butterflies on it), March 16, 1927- March 9, 2005, Forever our Angel, Deeply missed but never forgotten." We were so proud showing up with our T-shirts. I pray that next year the whole family will go. It would be a good way to honor Mom. Thelma was driving her car around in case any one was getting tired and needed a break or a ride back. We all started out together. Then Monica, Jade and Courtney went ahead and were running. I was in the middle all along. I needed the time to be by myself. I needed the thinking time. It had not been that long since Mom passed. One of the hospice workers stopped and asked me where my crew was. I said that no one wanted to walk with me. We got a chuckle out of it as I kept moving on. Chuck, Sheila, Paul and Blake finished up the hospice walk. We were cheering them on as they crossed the finish line. We made it the whole way, and I was so proud of everyone. We knew Mom was shining down on us, as proud as could be.

Living for the Moment

Chuck had so much determination to make it the whole way. He had been practicing the week before, walking a little bit each night. We live in a small town where everyone knows everybody, and they know Chuck is not normally a walker. People were stopping him and asking him what he was doing. He explained he was walking for the hospice fundraiser and it would cost the person ten dollars for asking him. Chuck raised a lot of money in the last few weeks.

When we were done walking, we stopped and had some water and treats. A guy came and told Chuck that he had won first place and a TV/DVD combo. We were all surprised that someone in our group won. They loaded it in Chuck's car. There was a little ten-year old that had just lost his grandma to cancer. He had found 49 sponsors, and Chuck had beat him by a few dollars. When we heard our group won, we all just stood there and looked at each other thinking the same thing. "What would Mom do?" Chuck called the guy over and told him to unload the TV and that he wanted to give it to the little boy who deserved it. The boy was so surprised that his hard work had paid off. They had their picture taken together. It was an emotional moment for all of us. Life is about giving. Mom was always giving. What a beautiful way to honor her today as we walk for hospice. Today was a day full of so many blessings. We all went out for lunch to celebrate Mom's life. Then we all went home to soak our feet. Because of what hospice did for our family, we will always support anything they do. We will find ways to help them as they helped us. We all embraced our jobs as caretakers. We did a good job but we could not have done that without the help of hospice and what they taught us. They always gave us the faith that we could do whatever needed to be done.

One week after our hospice walk, I just wanted to talk about Mom. I called the social worker, and we met at Mom's house. I did not have a key. We went in Mom's camper and had a visit. What a perfect place to talk about Mom—the camper she had spent so much time in. Things happen for a reason.

We sold Mom's camper to Barb and her sister. They are taking it to auctions and selling food. They have plans to put a yellow butterfly on it in memory of Mom. She must be so proud as she smiles down at them from auction to auction.

Brenda Ann Rebelein

Thursday, July 21, 2005

Dear God – Today is the day Mom and I planned for a long time. It is our pajama party today. This is the closure for us of our journey. My last wish to fulfill is my party. Please help me through the day. I know you and Mom will be watching us from above, giving us the wink that says we are all okay.

Two weeks ago, I sent out invitations based on Mom's guest list. I wrote a question mark to what kind of party it was. The location was at my campsite where we keep our camper. They all knew where that was. Someone had called me to find out more, but I would not give a clue. I told them just be ready to have some fun. I said I was getting things ready for my guests, talking to Mom, and letting her know I would make a good party for her just like she had planned. No one would expect a pajama party because it's 95 with no breeze. It was fun getting things ready. I had their gifts in little bags with their names on it. Mom's favorite foods were out in the screened-in porch. I had the wine coolers in a cooler next to the camper. I enjoyed being alone. This was my time to say a final goodbye to Mom as her final wish came true. My life would move on, but I would always cherish the time we had together the last few months.

I was finishing up the final touches for my party when I lost the use of my electricity, and so I had the park manager help me. We could not find the problem. I did not have anything extra plugged in to cause this. That was the puzzle. I called Mike and Josh, and they came to my rescue. I had arranged for someone to be my helper, so I could focus on my party. She arrived the same time Mike and Josh did. I was glad I had the food ready. We sat and waited until they could find the problem. We were laughing. It was Mom trying to pull the last joke on my party. Mike had to call the company of our camper. Our camper is brand new, so we should not be having problems. It took them three hours to find the problem. In the back of the camper three wires burnt out for no reason. This puzzled Mike and the person on the phone who helped us.

When we were sitting and waiting, my helper was laughing and pointing to the cooler. I had my wine coolers in. There was a butterfly hovering around the crack of the cooler. I laughed. "The butterfly may not be yellow, but I know it has to be Mom. She wants a wine cooler." We

162

Living for the Moment

watched the butterfly for awhile, and then the lights went on. When we turned, the butterfly was gone. I believe it was Mom saying thank you.

Our guests started to arrive. Everyone was so puzzled and confused when they got there. Some people knew each other and others did not. I could see they were nervous. It made me chuckle just thinking about how Mom would love this. What is this secret party? I had Mom's favorite foods set up and ready. There were just a few last minute items to get ready. My helper was busy, so I could greet my guests. They were offered a cool beverage. It was so hot and humid. But I think they were thinking about the party and not noticing the heat.

It was fun to see who would guess that it was a pajama party. I gave them their gift bags and their little sayings that went with them. We laughed and had fun with it. Look, Mom, no tears. We had our lunch. They all knew Mom had planned the meal when I was serving brownies and pickles together. They were all amazed Mom would plan such a party. We had our picture taken with our pajamas on. I was glad to have mine back. Every time I went to stay at Mom's she would grab them and keep them for herself. I had teased her that she was lucky I have a pajama addiction so I never ran out.

We had a good time together. The party could not have gone any better. The food was good, the company was fun, and the pajamas all fit. Mom planned a great party. I was so honored to give it for her. Everything that was here was Mom. Everyone went home early. Everything got cleaned up. The garbage got taken out. The guests were home tucked in their own beds with Mom smiling down at me knowing our party was a huge success.

I stayed overnight in my camper to say goodbye to Mom alone. This was our final night for wishes to come true. I wanted to enjoy the moment. I had waited months to have this party, and no one knew but Mom and me. It was sad coming to the end. I live with no regrets. I hold my head up high. I did the best for Mom. *I talk to you now. I know it is time to say goodbye until we meet again. I will put you to rest. It is time for me to move on. I will not forget. Thanks for helping me grow up and become the mom I always wanted to be. I got the honor to take care of you. We had so many fun days, and the bad days were only moments that have gone away. It was a learning experience. You showed me how to die with dignity and pride.* God Bless our guardian angel, Marvel Mae.

163

Brenda Ann Rebelein

I could not end my book without telling one more story. Darcy, Jade, Megan, and I have a yearly bike trail riding weekend together. When Mom was alive she went along and sat in the camper and read all day while we were gone. This year things were not going right. We had to cancel our plans. We had no reservations and everything was full. Darcy called 25 places to find us a place to stay, but she was having no luck. We were all feeling blue, so Darcy decided to try one more time. She found a little lavender house for rent. She had nothing to lose, so she called it. They had 115 calls from people wanting to rent this house and fifteen minutes before Darcy called, the party that had it rented for the weekend canceled. Darcy rented it for the weekend. Mom's favorite color is lavender. We left early the next morning. We wondered whether Mom sent us the little lavender house since she was not with us any more. When we got there, we were so excited. It was so cute. It looked like a place Mom would love to stay. We walked into a little porch, then into a little living room to the right. When you come in, there is a bedroom. I heard Darcy laugh. I looked at the bedroom and all I could see was butterflies—on the wall, the bedspread, the pillowcases and the picture. "Oh, you guys, Grandma beat us here!" I screamed. We laughed until we had tears coming down our faces. It was another one of those special moments.

The following poems I wrote during mom's cancer journey. She read most of them during our time together. She insisted I hang them around the house including the poems the grandchildren wrote. The pictures they drew from their heart. I never studied poetry. It came from the heart as times it can be overwhelming. God was good to me, he let me walk when I had the strength and carried me when I needed a friend.

Brenda Ann Rebelein

MARVEL, OUR MOM AND GRANDMA

Mom—what a big word.
Our mom is named Marvel Mae Bartlet Niebuhr. And what a lady!
The fondest memory I have of my mom is when she had the
    restaurant.
She had won $200.00 worth of groceries at the market.
"I do not want that," she replied in her loud voice,
which we have all heard at times.

She wanted it to go to one of the families in Freeborn
who had no food to spare.
On Christmas Day, no one gets to eat
until the people who have no families have been fed.
That was our mom.
She had a heart of gold.
She was a woman with a lot of class.

If there were more people in this world like our mom,
we would live in a better place.
Chuck, Bruce, Darcy and I are lucky to say she's our mom.
Thelma, Wendy, Jeremy and Mike are gifted to get a prized mother-
    in-law.
And the grandchildren, when they are hungry or want to run away
because they think no one understands,
they know Grandma Marvel's is the place to go.

Mom, you taught us your best.
Thank you, Mom, for a job well done.
Good-bye, Mom.
We know that it is time for you to leave,
to enjoy your eternal rest.
Lord, watch over her, as she did us.
We will all be ready for heaven some day,
but is heaven really ready for Marvel Mae?

God, if you want a perfect angel, one is on her way.

Living for the Moment

MOM, I LOVE YOU!

Dearest Mom,
You have given me lots of memories to remind me of you.
We will be okay.
South Dakota, Morton trips, Christmas, and everyday will not be the
    same.
But what is the same is….
You have given me strength, courage and love.
My phone bill will go down sadly.
And no one can set me straight like you.
You have given to so many people.
No one can cook as well as you, as we have all been told.
I will stay strong.
What will I do without you?
I will make sure you have pretty flowers at your gravesite.
I can not be angry.
I will have my journals to keep me warm.
This is not our choice.
I say thank you for all you've done.
I will keep a smile on my face.
See, Mom. No tears.
I have to thank God for sharing you with us for so many years.
So, good luck. We will see you soon.
We will have Charlie to keep us intact, so now wish us luck.
Have a good time on your journey.
I just have three words to say, Mom—
I love you!

Brenda Ann Rebelein

THOSE WERE SOME GOOD YEARS

Our lives have changed so suddenly, and we have no control.
It is time to leave our lives to a higher power, as He knows best.
We had good times and bad.

I take back when I was a teenager
and I thought you were rather dumb.
Now you seem rather smart.

You and dad have taught us how to work.
Dad did the plumbing at Eberts and then at Jim and Dude's.
And you were the best bartender Roger Ille has ever known.

And boy, how mad you would get
when Dad would sneak off with his friends instead of work.
When Roger's closed, you wanted restaurant work.

We got the M&M Café, and boy, did we have fun.
And then on to bigger and better things—
we started Club 90 bar and restaurant.

We had many years of hard work, as it was family owned.
Dad was in charge of slicing (he thought he was the best).
Then came the meat runs, and what town did he go to?

Mom, you were the best teacher of the restaurant business.
You taught me all that I know,
even though I still hear you hollering,

"Brenda, where did you go? The tables are wrong,
chairs don't go there, you dummy."
The Prime Rib and BBQ Rib parties were outstanding.

You showed us what you had.
Dad got sick and met his higher power as he got called home.
Then all things have to come to an end.

Living for the Moment

No more Club 90, and oh, what a loss.
Time for you to enjoy yourself
because you have worked so hard.
After a few months had passed
and it was hard for you to be alone
and you missed being with people,

You got all dressed up, and I thought you found a man.
"No, for God sakes, I'm getting a job," you said.
"Hello, Mom, has anyone told you that you're 64?"

You went to Café Don'E and then to HyVee.
Kitchens are where you feel at home.
But now it is time to start a kitchen in heaven.

With you serving Prime Rib and BBQ Ribs,
No one will go unfed.
So enjoy yourself and take the reins.

We called ahead to let them know.
The peace in heaven is about to erupt.
Marvel Mae is on her way.

Brenda Ann Rebelein

A PLACE CALLED HOME

What does a family home really mean?
Mom and Dad built this home from scratch
To raise a family they had always dreamed of.

We all came here as babies,
And here had our first steps.
The teenage years we were testing the waters.
The tears we had through growing up.
We all brought the loves of our lives here to get your approval.
Then came the grandchildren, and they grew up so fast.

Our home is where everyone comes
when you have good news to share,
or just to say hi.
Mom's door has always been open.

And if we can not see through a situation,
Mom will say, "Now think."
Our answer was there all along,
but it took mom to show us the way.

The dining room table has seen and heard every thing.
Even the hidden cigarettes.
Our home has had the best Christmas parties one could ever dream.
As the family got bigger each year with more babies,
the fireplace filled up with pictures.

We have laughed, cried, and played jokes as this is home.
How many meals has Mom prepared in this little kitchen?
From children, adults, and strangers to hobos,
we all benefited from the good food.

Nothing is better than going home.
We are so lucky to say our special place is Home

Living for the Moment

GRANDMA, WE LOVE THE SAME

Marvel loved her grandchildren; there was never a doubt.
You should have seen the smile on her face
when she found out another member of the family
was to be born in the Niebuhr clan.

Mom could not wait to get that new little one
on the dining room table to love and to cuddle with.
And the funny things
they used to do when they learned to walk.

As they all got older, they all wanted to stay at grandma's house.
It was a fun place to be.
So they all had to take their turns, or grandma would throw her
    hands up
and say, "Fine you all can stay."

There were the grocery trips,
fishing in Alden Lake
and going with grandma in her camper
and having a cookout.

And don't forget her birthday party at Jackpot Junction
in Morton. Oh, what a blast.
How many grandchildren ran away to grandma's house,
as she was the only one who understands.

She would take them in
and then spread their wings,
and let them have their fun.
Slowly, she had a talk with them

whether they were right and wrong.
More fun was ahead.
That was what they needed—a friend.
Mom and Dad got a talking too.

171

Brenda Ann Rebelein

Grandma sent them home to Mom and Dad
and all was love and warm. They all had it at grandma's house.
A place to go for encouragement and to know you were loved
for who you are. And for someone to say "now think"

Weddings were always so much fun for Grandma
As she loved her blue dress. Before we all dreaded it,
but now we love the blue dress
as it hangs so peacefully behind the closet door.
With our cancer journey starting, Grandma can't get enough
of the little ones. Parents being protective,
"Be careful, don't make a mess." Grandma always saying,
"Let them be. They're not hurting a thing."

There was a day when grandma stared out her bedroom window,
"Do you think my grandchildren know how much I love them?"
I got goosebumps and said,
"Yes, they do, Grandma, because they love you the same."

Living for the Moment

JUST FOR TODAY

Mom, you give me strength
and courage to go on each day.
I pray for you every day
as this horrible disease controls our lives.

I love your smile and your evil laugh.
You make life durable, and this will pass.
I have learned from you
that we need to live just for today.

I'm so grateful to get the chance
to take care of you, enjoying
all the days we have left together,
and I will cherish each moment.

God will take care of us,
as this is all in His hands.
Let us, your kids, give to you
what you have given us all these years.

I would change places with you
in a New York minute, if that was possible.
But we do not hold the future
as we pray for the best.

I will enjoy your good moments
and help you with the bad.
And I know that we will all be okay.
God will be by our side.

We will take one day at a time.
And keep hoping for tomorrows.
I know you tire easily now,
so lay back down. It is time to rest.

Brenda Ann Rebelein

We will take the good days
and have some laughs as you order us around.
Because we know you do it the best.
Things will be fine with your kids by your side.

This is so much harder than one can say.
We used to see this strong, vibrant woman
ready to take on the world.
Now, it is so hard to see you so frail and helpless.

But you know we are by your side
and we live just for today.
The past is behind us.
Our future is not here.

And the present is so precious.
We will be here for the good and the bad,
the days ahead. Know that you are loved
by your family so dear.

I live my life each morning thinking, *Just for today.*

Living for the Moment

God, I know You're here giving me a sign.

Where are You? Hear my prayer!
We take each day as it has been given.
Today was a hard one to bear.
Mom is crying and calling Your name.
God, You seem to be elsewhere.
I need to learn to wait my turn.
"Help me, help me," is what we hear.
You give us nothing more then what we can bear.
The pain seems to be so unbearable.
As we hold mom in our arms.
Nothing seems to help.
God, we are here. Do You care?
Hours have gone by.
It seems to me.
Mom opens her eyes,
And says. "Thank God, I'm pain free."
We are sorry we doubted Your work.
So for now we say "Thank You, God."
I will try and keep my patience up.
Till You say. "Come my child, Marvel Mae,
let Me lead you on the way."

Brenda Ann Rebelein

Mom, I'm So Scared

I'm so scared today.
There is nowhere to hide.
The days are getting longer.
One hour at a time seems too long.
I have prayed so hard today
As this will come to an end.
The smile on your face has left you.
And now it is a jerk of pain.
The medication has been a trick,
Causing you to be chatty most of the time.
It kills me to see you suffer.
I know God is near
And always carrying us through.
I try to leave Him to his work.
As we watch, you whittle away.
Your feet are cold, the purple is near!
Your eyes cry for help
With you not shedding a tear.
You pick at your covers.
As it must be a comfort
I wish I could hold you and never let you go.
And take all the pain away.
God, help us! And make it all go away.

Living for the Moment

Pajama Party to Remember

I'm proud of me. I did not cry; I held my head up so high.
Mom asked me long ago,
"It will not be long when I cannot think for myself. I have a plan to
    help you mend.
Take my pajamas and have a good time. This is the food list and
    don't forget the wine. The guests will not know what they are
    there for, so don't say a word. Put on a smile and take care. Your
    camper is the place you need to be, as you know camping meant
    the world to me."
My guests arrived with puzzled looks.
"Okay, Brenda what are we here for?"
"Sit down and relax," I did reply.
We had a toast to good memories; they all received their gift bag.
When they saw what was in the bag, they knew Mom had struck
    again.
They all put on their pajamas that meant so much to Mom.
She had a saying that went with each bag.
It was hot and humid with no breeze in sight.
"Put on your pajamas and smile pretty, and don't look so uptight."
The lunch was good.
The wine was great.
We saw a butterfly that wanted to join our site.
We knew it must be our Marvel Mae.
It flew away knowing we were all safe and having a good time.
"Mom, look we are all okay."
It was a great party and lots of laughs.
I'm glad Mom planned this party for me to give.
This was what our gal was like—good food, good friends.
A piece of work God did just right

Brenda Ann Rebelein

Thank You, God, For the Time Well Spent

God, I think of you today as every day when I start my daily prayer.
As the memories of Mom float through my head.
It is one of those days I miss her so much.
I need to think of the fun we had.
The time we spent together.
Since Mom had come home from the hospital, she made each day
    full of hope. The jokes each day she wanted to play, keeping the
    positive outlook as this is the way it was suppose to be.
The coffee is on, and go get more cookies.
We've got company once again.
It was fun to stop in and see how the day is going. Or just to visit to
    say hi.
Let's meet at Mom's and pile in her little bedroom. We have room for
    one more.
Mom is smiling and looking her best.
Time was moving on.
The pain was increasing.
Mom taught me how to take life just as you get it.
Don't worry about the small stuff, as it always seems to work out.
We got the closet cleaned out. Things in their place.
The basement was her domain; she loved going down there,
    remembering when she and Dad built the house from scratch.
Mom loved to dust and rearrange her flowers as she thought of the
    good times.
So many things got done, and families' wishes are coming true as we
    get these keepsakes to remember a great lady.
This all happened on the cancer journey.
If there was an accident and she was taken away,
We would not have gotten this time well spent.

Living for the Moment

Happy Mother's Day, Mom!

Today is our special day.
God made us moms.
I wish you a good day today. Even though we are apart,
our hearts intertwine forever.
I miss you today, but, Mom, I'm doing just fine.
Grandma Sophia and you get to spend time together.
Mom and daughter, once again.
Just the way it used to be.
I think of all our Mother's Days together, working side by side.
Those memories keep warm and put a smile on my face.
Some things I will never forget. I will always be your daughter,
I'm so lucky to say I had a special mom.
I know you will have a good time with your great attitude,
smile, and warm heart.
Tell Grandma hi and that I send my love.
Happy Mother's Day from my heart!

Love ya Mom, Brenda

Brenda Ann Rebelein

Camping Time: A Talk With Mom

As I sit out here at Pihls Park.
I think of what could have been.
Chuck and you came up with a new idea.
"Get a camper, we will get together and have so much fun. We can
    sneak off and camp
when everyone is too busy."
The camper was bought; we all were excited as can be.
But God had different plans for us.
He needed your help being one of his angels.
As he called her home.
Now I sit here all alone.
You taught me how much fun camping is. Playing is just as important
    as working hard.
All the meals that her camper served and don't forget the BBQ Ribs.
How many women would make forty-seven pounds of Ribs out of a
    camper?
No one but our Marvel Mae.
So you need to live in us a little longer as we try and remember your
    cooking tricks.
We will do our best and have a good laugh when we sit with a mess.
I sit here listening to the birds.
Enjoying the peace and quiet.
It is suppertime now. The families are having a good time getting
    things set up.
We both loved to read. You with your romance and me with my
    mysteries.
One thing is we never saw eye to eye on our reading.
The big thing we agreed on is family time.
You will be missed this camping season and years to come.
Just send us a sign you're doing okay.
As you enjoy your campsite in heaven up above.

Living for the Moment

Making New Memories.

Today is the day we sign the house away.
We pass down our memories to a new family.
Mom's final wish is coming true today.
Monica and Chad are buying the house.
The day mom was called home to God,
Monica met up with an old school friend named Chad.
We feel Mom sent him her way from above.
They have become quite a couple, with a ring on her finger to show.
Desiree and Destiny will have a place to call home. The future is
    looking good for them.
Mom would be so proud and smiling down at us.
The house will be filled once again with laughter, tears and bruised
    up knees.
When we did our packing, our memories came along.
Take care, Mom and Dad we loved this house.
Years will come and go and parties will never be the same.
It is time to make new memories.
Grandma will be missed but she is happy that we have moved on.
To our little family this house is yours.
Keep it up with pride now that Grandma's wish came true.
Grandma had faith in you, as her children we stand behind you.
Build new memories with the girls.
They go to school now so far away, just like we did many years ago.
Family and friends will come and go. Have fun in this house, it is a
    nice little house.
Some day you may live alone. Or maybe another grandchild will be
ready to say "I'll take Grandma's house."
Our work is done as this all comes to the end.
The house has been sold and not a tear in my eye.
So grateful Mom's dream has become a reality.
I feel her close by.
See, Mom, wishes do come true.

Brenda Ann Rebelein

MY OLDEST FRIEND

By Josh Rebelein, 6th grade, 2001

My oldest friend is Marvel Mae Bartlet Niebuhr. Marvel is my grandma, and she is 75 years old. I feel she is the best older person anyone would want for a friend. She always takes good care of me. My grandma helps me when I'm sick or having a bad day.

Since I was little I have went to her house and spent time with her. Sometimes we have a house full and then the best time is when it is she and I. Then I don't have to share my grandma with anyone.

One Easter we all went to grandmas and we had an Easter Hunt. She told me where the best eggs were hiding. When I go to my grandma's I get to plan the menu. It is always pizza. My grandma is the best cooker in the world. She use to own her own restaurant. I'm proud of my grandma she is not retired. She works at HyVee.

My grandma likes to play cards with me. We usually play golf and blackjack 21. I like to spend the night over to her house. My last birthday she let me have a party at her house and she invited my cousin's and we had a blast. The boy's were the football players and the girl's were the cheerleader's and when we came in grandma's house we had a 4-course meal a 6th grader would die for. When I'm at grandma's house one thing she tells me is "Cleanup your mess."

When she is hungry for bullheads I have to go to Alden with my fishing pole and catch her a meal of bullheads. The she fry's them up and she gives me the tails. My grandma takes me camping in her camper. A bee stung me and she took good care of me. We have had a lot of good times in her camper. My grandma teaches me right from wrong and she is always there for me when I need a friend or just someone to hang around with. She is the coolest grandma anyone would want to have. My friend.

Living for the Moment

"Free my Grandma and let her stay."

God, please don't take my grandma from me. Get rid of the cancer
and set her free.
Cancer is the devil, and it's not fair. The pain my heart makes me
wish I did not care.
Marvel Mae Niebuhr is not only my grandma, she is my friend.
Without her, my heart would never mend.
Of the family she is the rock. Why did this all have to come as a
shock?
I will have a career. Wedding and children someday.
For this I want my grandma to stay.
My grandma's house has always been a second home for me.
In the future, this is still the way I want it to be.
How I wish her life would never end,
because of her hands, mouth and ears she always has to lead.
Part of me will always be missing if she's not here and death will
remain my biggest fear.
To me….. An angel, my grandma Marvel will always and forever be.

I love you Grandma
Always and forever
Your granddaughter Tessa
{Bruce and Wendy's daughter}

Brenda Ann Rebelein

Good-bye to my Angel

I have been an aide for many years.
To see you in this condition brings me to so many tears.
I watch you laying there in your bed grabbing at the air.
For all you do is look past me and stare.
I know all the signs that are to come ahead.
Before you know it, It will have you dead.
Nothing in all the years of my training prepared me.
To see you so lost and vulnerable and not able to be.
All of your family members are going to grow up fast.
For all the youngsters you will be the thing of the past.
But I do promise this- they'll never forget all your love.
That great grandma Marvel will always be looking from above.
Apnea, pain and sudden incontience was hard to bare.
All I could do was step up and showed I care.
It was hard to just sit and let you go without such a good-bye.
Seeing you sleeping there in your bed I did not even cry.
For you grabbed my hand and whispered "Monica is that really you?
For I'm dreaming and can't see what is even true.
Take good care of my house the best you can.
For one day you will be happy with a very good man.
For making lots of memories so await all three of you.
Now I can rest in peace and know my dream has finally come true"

Monica Rebelein
[Our daughter Monica]

Grandma

Grandma, you were always there for comfort, and in times of need.
You were always saying times would be all right, when you knew they
   wouldn't be.
It's hard to say "I love you," because I know I do not express it well.
I already know how you feel, I hope you know how I do as well.
It is crazy how the world changes from day to day.

I remember when I was learning to drive with you, grandma and
   grandpa. You were in
the backseat.
You did not seem nervous at all, even when I came close to the ditch.
Grandpa said I was doing alright, and you said "Aww heck she is
   doing great."
You knew I could handle it, and I was just perfect.

You try to help everyone, others would think that is crazy.
Most would just help their own family, but not you.
You help everyone who needed it the most.
Everyone loved you, you were so sweet.
When someone would do something stupid, You would say "You
   dummy."
Those were the gold ol' days, funny, yet true.
All I know right now is that I'm really missing you!

I really miss those days, now that you are gone.
I can not believe they just took you away from us. Into heaven above.
But grandpa has been waiting. I know that is true.
He just couldn't wait, till he could be with you.
He has been gone for so long, leaving you behind.
He left back in the year of 1991.
I never got to know him; I was all but only 3.
Now you are both gone, into the heavens up above watching over
   me.

Brenda Ann Rebelein

Well, grandma, I'm glad that you were in my life.
I got to spend so many years with you; I had such a wonderful time.
I miss you dearly, you were the best neighbor, and the BEST
  grandma too.
Just never forget me. Because I will never forget you.
I just want you to know...

"I love you"
By Courtney
Sheila's daughter
Chuck and Thelma's
Granddaughter

Living for the Moment

Marvel Mae Niebuhr

It has been a year since you passed away.
But your memories are with us every single day.
Sometimes I still lie awake and begin to cry.
Asking the good Lord why you had to die.
He sent us a baby girl who looks just like you.
    so you're always with us in everything we do.
A picture of you I have on my wall, to
    remind me of the love you shared with us all.
I'll love your forever, my Grandma Marvel Mae.
    wishing you were here in every way.
Although you're not by me to talk and to share, I know
You are watching because I know hoe much you care.
So whenever I'm lonely or even feel blue, I just
    remember you're watching and I love you, too.

Love, Jeremy, Aurora, Mayson Lee and Cearra Mae
[Bruce and Wendy's daughter and family]

Brenda Ann Rebelein

Dr. Mohr, Mom's Doctor and Friend

Thinking of you so often,
as the days all go on.
Marvel was your patient and your friend.
As you go back 20 years,
You have joked and had many good reports.
Even you wasted your breath. Mom would laugh if you mentioned a
    diet.
You always replied with a sigh "You as so healthy; you must be doing
    something right.
So keep up the good work and we will see you at your next physical."
The day came that you did dread.
You had to tell your patient and your friend.
"Marvel you have the big C."
We had seen the lump in your throat.
Knowing these are the days you do dread.
You promised mom you would keep her comfortable, as she does not
    have
Much time left.
Mom held her head up high.
and told us we will not cry.
We brought her home and did our best.
Mom made us laugh and enjoy life.
And remember we are living just for today.
When things were slipping with cancer progressing.
I asked her, "Mom are you scared?"
She paused a moment or two and said, "If I was scared, I did not
    know how to live."
There was a day she asked what was wrong with her.
"Mom you have cancer." I did reply.
"I know" she said and drifted off for a few minutes. "Call Dr. Mohr,
    he knows what's wrong with me. We will go to Rochester, Mayo
    Clinic, and 4th floor, the Baldwin Building. He always take care
    of me."
Mom passed away peacefully as she prayed for.
We want to thank you for all the care and good heart you showed our

Living for the Moment

Mom, grandma, and friend.
She loved you so. She loved to tease you and thought you were the
best.
She was an outstanding lady with a lot of class.
We will always remember what you did for your patient and friend.
God bless you for being the doctor you are.
Mom taught us to live life to the fullest.
And she showed us how to die with dignity and pride.
Thank you again from the Niebuhr Clan.

Brenda Ann Rebelein

To Hospice Staff and Volunteers

On September 1st the Niebuhr family's lives changed.
On September 15th a program named hospice entered our lives.
They took over. We were so powerless as cancer had taken over our
    mom, Marvel Mae.
The staff of hospice set up the house so we could keep Mom at
    home.
The nurses and all the others helped us each day,
And all the others who answered our calls.
Mom was blessed with so many wonderful people to help her out.
She would have never met them if cancer had not knocked on her
    door.
From the nurses, the staff, and bath ladies to the volunteers—
We love you and Thank you for this ride.
There were good days and bumpy roads, but a call to hospice to hear
    a calm voice saying
"It will be okay."
You never judged us for what we were doing.
You walked us through and let us know we were never alone.
For this, we will always be grateful and care so much.
You saw us all getting tired and sent us the earth angels, the
    volunteers.
Our plan to keep Mom home was only a dream.
You helped this be fulfilled.
We got our second wind.
God saw Mom's weary eye as this was a difficult path.
She took part of us with her,
As part of us will always be with hospice care.
If the world had more people like hospice caregivers, this would be a
    better world.

Thank you for all you help and concerns.
The family of Marvel Mae Niebuhr
Hospice care from September 15TH 2004-March 9th 2005

Living for the Moment

Ruth, Our Friend, Bath Lady and Special Companion

Ruth, I think of you as an angel on this earth.
We go back many years.
You came to us with a special deed
When we faced this cancer journey.
You stepped up and took care of our mom.
You will always be our special bath lady.
We love your smile and your friendly greeting.
There are not enough words to say thank you.
God made special people like you.
Your job choice is to go to peoples home that can not do for
    themselves any more.
What can we give you in return?
    A special place in heaven is what you deserves.
Mom gave a smile when she knew it was Ruthie Day.
You would come on the good days and bad.
You always talked and made us feel better.
We would look to see when you would come next,
Knowing that would be a good day.
All the girls do a good job, but Ruth and mom had a great
    connections
You put her heart and soul in your work, and always gave it your all.
Ruth, you taught us many things about care- giving that will stay
    with us all.
You had that little giggle and smile as big as can be.
You always had a plan if a change had to be.
Mom says no one can give a bath like that Ruthie gal.
Mom loved to look pretty. As appearance was a big thing.
You gave the bath, got the makeup; hair was ready for the week,
    never had enough
hairspray get another can.
You would sit mom in her chair and say. "There, Marvel you are
    ready for the day."
    So thank you Ruth and give yourself a pat on the back for a job
    well done.
Keep up the good work, as the Niebuhr Clan will never forget.

Brenda Ann Rebelein

Chuck, My Brother

Thanks for being a big brother I look up to and will never forget.

We did a good job with mom and paid her back for what she did for
all of us.

I'm glad I could count on you to help mom's wishes come true.

We had fun and lots of jokes, mom loved to get us together for a
battle or two

when she could sit back and giggle to see what we would do.

I'm glad you and mom fulfilled her wish to hand down her secret
BBQ Sauce,

The fighting you two did to get it made just right.

We will make sure things stay the same even though mom was our
rock.

Watch for the yellow butterfly because she is watching you.

Living for the Moment

Bruce, My Brother

I'm glad we got to take care of mom together as this was her wish.
Thanks for answering all my calls when I needed a hand.
We did a good job as we did what needed to be done.
We have lots of memories to think about.
It was fun watching you and mom playing cards to see who was
     cheating? I think
you both were giving it your best shot.
You will always be my brother so what do you think of that?
I know you do not believe, but that yellow butterfly is checking up
     on you.

Brenda Ann Rebelein

Darcy, My Sister

We have made quite a team!
I knew I loved you, but now I know I love you more.
It is sad we had to lose our mom.
To become so close.
But I have always been told there are some good days with the bad.
I knew you were a call away.
We did a good job with mom.
She would be so proud.
So pat yourself on the back.
With a job well done.
Our families have suffered.
We have missed them so.
Our life is back.
And mom is safe.
Thank you for being a sis and a friend.
I will promise you and pinky promise.
I will take care of you until the end.
Mom left us each with many memories to hold tight.
She will smile down at us.
As a pretty yellow butterfly or a dragonfly.

Mike, My Husband

Mike, you know what you mean to me I will love you forever.
You need to know I will never forget you letting me live with my
    mom.
I stepped aside from our business that means so much to us.
You thought of us when it was time to eat and showed you care.
I would call and I tell we would need this or that, and you would be
    on your way.
Then when mom got bad, you wanted to stay.
You chipped in where a lot of men would not do.
 How do I thank you?
We are partners at home and at work.
Taking care of mom, we made a good team.
The day you held my mom and reassured her she would be okay,
Was the day I fell in love with you all over again.
I will take care of you forever; now you know you're a lucky man.
I know how hard you worked to get mom's wish to come true.
The time is coming real soon when Monica is the proud owner of
    grandma's house.
And who knows, someday there maybe another grandchild that will
    say,
"I can live in grandma's house, the house they built many years ago."
You have been so patient when I needed my space.
I know you and Josh enjoyed your bachelor pad, but momma is
    home.
One more time thanks for all you have done.
I love you more my friend.
You helped me through the days teaching me to be strong to take
    care of my mom.
It was fun having her as my patient, but it was better when she was
    my mom.
I will always remember this cancer journey as you had faith in me.
We will grow old together and take care of each other knowing we
    both have
a soft place to fall.
You are my hero, husband and friend.

Brenda Ann Rebelein

Jeanette, My Cousin and Friend

Jeanette, you married my cousin years ago.
I saw you in passing, not knowing how you would steal my heart.
You have been a friend to my mom.
And hold those memories tight.
You two hold your secrets that no one needs to know.
Mom saw you through your marriage and the death of a son.
Grab her strength and always stay strong.
Buck up and don't be a wimp.
It's what she would want you to do.
You faced this cancer journey, as we had no control.
You set your family aside.
To take care of a friend.
You cared, you baked and did your best.
Never forget how much you're loved.
Mom went to a better place.
She is our guardian angel by our side.
She will see us and be missed.
We will go camping and keep her close.
To laugh and cry is okay.
Thank you for all you have done.
Keep the chin up and enjoy your life.
As we all move on.
Give yourself credit, as it was well deserved.
You are my cousin and my friend.

Living for the Moment

Our Aunt, Companion, Helper and Friend, Mary Lou

Mary Lou, how does one say thank you in a million ways?
Your life has changed as cancer has changed all of ours.
We thank you for only being a call away.
You have cooked, cleaned, and been a helper to our mom.
No one can forget you being a friend.
You stayed with mom and helped us out.
It means a lot to us that you help us with our pain.
As we crossed those bridges we did not know the future.
I pray that some day, we can be by your side to help you in any way.
Once again, We want to thank you in a million ways.
So keep the chin up!
And remember you're loved.
Your kindness has been appreciated every day.
There is a special place in heaven for special people like you.
This is for your sister Marvel Mae.
You hold your own memories as we do.
Keep them close to your heart.
As we go down this path of the unknown.
May God bless you and your courage, kindness, and strength.

Brenda Ann Rebelein

Candy, Our Beautician

Only our hairdresser knows for sure.
Mom and you had a wonderful companionship.
You told her and she told you.
Mom loved the Candy days when it was her excuse to cook.
Candy loves this so fix her a plate.
Never forget how much she loved you.
Mom was your customer and your friend.
Then came the day we all did dread.
The big C word became our life.
You took the time to take care of mom.
"I need more hair spray, I lost my brush. Don't forget I need more
    color for my hair."
    As you showed her your best.
She gave it a check mark that was always A plus.
We will never forget you coming to the house.
With your smile, laughter, and readiness to work.
Mom loved you as you loved her.
Hang onto those memories on those days.
As we all wish we had more of Marvel Mae.
Part of us went with her.
When she was called home.
I pray as you do too that heaven has enough hair supplies for your
    Marvel Mae.
Look for the beautiful yellow butterfly as it is combed just right.
Thank you Candy for helping our mom and grandma
We know you did it for you, too.
She was a special lady.
Thanks for going on the call of duty and being our friend.
It will always be remembered and kept close to our heart.

Living for the Moment

Barb, Our Singer

I need to say thank you and shed a tear.
Mom and I enjoyed your music through our cancer journey.
It always made us feel better and calmed our hearts.
You made us so happy the day of the funeral.
When you came with your voice and ready to sing.
Mom was shinning down on us.
On the day her new life began.
You were a hard act to follow when I had to read my poem.
But I had my orders as you did too.
Make this say a special service.
Mom would say to you, "Oh. Barb, you did such a good job."
As the lady we will always remember as Marvel Mae.
You have laughed, cried and had many good times.
The family can not say thank you enough.
I have played your music over and over.
Nashville is where you should be.
We wish you a lifetime of happiness what you deserve
I will always remember your words on the tape. "Marvel, boy, we
    sure hope this works."
And how those words comforted us many days.
So thank-you, dear Barb! We love you so.
You helped us give mom the send off she deserved.
So God bless you, as it had to be hard.
You put your feelings aside and gave it your all.
Your friend Marvel was watching you.
Some day you will see the beautiful yellow butterfly.
Knowing it is your friend Marvel Mae.

The songs that Barb sang were
"What a friend we have in Jesus."
"One Day at a Time."
[She customized it to fit our family with the camping,
fishing and Mom's good cooking and remember the good times]
"Dark Clouds."

199

Brenda Ann Rebelein

To my family and friends

I want to thank you for all you did.
Thanks for working a shift, stopping in for a visit and your calls.
I think of the time we had together with mom.

It puts a smile on my face.
The years we had together were fun.
The last seven months were the best.

Enjoy your memories, hold the tight.
Everyone helped with the laughter filled the house with joy.
Mom showed us all it was okay to die.

I love you all. I enjoyed every day we had spent together.
As we circle around our Marvel Mae.
One lesson I learned from mom.
Enjoy your time with your family and friends.

Make the best out of each moment.
Laughter is the best medicine.
Share a joke or two.

When you think of mom, keep her close to your heart.
God bless you for what you did for our mom, grandma and friend.

I Miss My Mom Today

Today is a tough one mom as I miss you so.
I need your strength to hang on tight.
I miss your smile; your wicked laugh and your humor that made me
    smile each day.
I asked God to relieve you from your pain. I can not take it back.
There is only one way for the pain to go away.
Heaven is the place we will all be some day.
No pain, no pills and cancer from above.
I need to think of what you went through; do not dwell on the pain.
How hard it was for us each day.
Mainly, for my patient Marvel Mae.
You were my mom and that is okay.
The long hours and the medication every two hours.
Calls to hospice, as we do not understand.
They bring a new drug we will try this or let's added a little more to
    give us a bump.
All the time we still stayed strong.
I wonder, were you scared? Or just brave for us?
God was there we know that.
We had six good months of fun, games, visitors and good meals.
The only bad was the last few weeks while God prepared you to walk
    with him.
Waffles will be served with a smile when we remember when.
There will always be a hole in my heart.
Till I meet my mom again.
I wait for the phone to ring, and then I stop and think mom is okay.
But for now I will try and stay strong and be grateful for what we
    had.
It is that I miss my mom.
I will think of the good times and be grateful for the moments.
The cancer can not take this away.
Stay strong, as this is what mom needs for me to be.
There is no more pain. Just a lifetime of happiness and smiling
    sunshine that she deserves.

Brenda Ann Rebelein

New Beginnings

Mom, it has been a year today since God called your name
to come "Home."
You can see we are all doing okay.
The grandchildren are growing and running about.
You would be proud of us all.

We promised you we would all get along. You gave us the tools.
Beginnings without you are things we are getting use too.
Our hearts are breaking and missing you.
But look mom "no tears."

You are my hero and my friend. I pray that someday I can be
strong like you.
We have all received your signs you have sent us so keep
them coming.
Then we know your doing okay.
I often wonder if you won a dance contest in
heaven just like you had planned.

Knowing my mom, you did your best.
New beginnings without you are hard. Like you told
us life goes on.
We have the memories of your good cooking,
camping and fishing.
As we live One day at a Time.

I promised you I would stay strong and have faith things
happen for a reason. God just needed the best.
As I smile with you on your one-year mark today.
I lay flowers here with you; it's time for me to go.
Mom, you know that I will come back.

Living for the Moment

Have a good day, mom.
Your new beginning started one-year ago today.

Love you forever until we meet again.
    Your daughter, Brenda

Author's Notes

This has been a beautiful journey. I can not say that enough. When people mention my mom, I just want to smile. I do not feel bad. We had a good time. We made the best with what we had. We received the news, and Mom taught us how to live with what time she had left, have fun, and not dwell on what we want. It was about acceptance. We stepped up to the plate and did what we had to do. I never dreamt I could do the things I did. When you love someone and want to repay him or her for all they did for you ... well, thinking about that, I knew I could do it. I did not think about it. I just wanted this for Mom. We made it happen. It was nice she could stay in her own home.

I remember the day she looked at me and said, "Brenda, it is coming soon, when I will not talk any more. Keep writing. Won't it be something if we could help just one person? Oh, what a blessing that would be." Then she closed her eyes and went to sleep. She wanted us all to remember her how she was. I wrote about the good days and the bad. I could not sugar coat this cancer journey because it was a long, hard road. If you hang in there, you can do it too. I would not give up. I knew we were close to having to move Mom out of her home. I just kept asking God, "God, keep us strong one more day." He always answered me when I needed to be carried or when I could walk my baby steps, but I never walked alone.

I still work with my husband Mike and son Josh. We have two weddings coming up—our daughter Monica and her fiancée Chad, they love their new home, and our son Lance and his fiancée Kristine. Monica and Chad were blessed with a son Cole Allen Sept. 26, 2006 at 7:32 p.m. weighing 7 pounds. Lance and Kristine will be marrying soon. Josh has a few years at home. Desiree and Destiny, Monica's children, are growing fast.

Chuck and Thelma are enjoying camping life, and spending time with their grandchildren. Vicki and husband Pete and family reside in Owatonna. Sheila and husband Paul and family still reside next to Monica and Chad and girls. Bruce and Wendy have two new granddaughters. Miranda and Tim had a girl named Payton Rose on August 23, 2005 at 3:13, weighing 7 lbs. 1 oz., and 20 inches long. Aurora and Jeremy also had a girl named Cearra Mae [named after

Grandma Marvel Mae] on Sept 25, 2005 at 6:39 weighing 8 lbs. 12oz and 21 inches long. Tessa and her fiancée Nathaniel will be having a wedding soon. Spenser still lives at home. Darcy and Jeremy went to LasVegas to renew their marriage vows at CircusCircus where they got married the first time. We know Mom was with them in spirit. Jade and Megan still live at home. The grandchildren are busy with raising their families. Jim and Jeanette's son and daughter-inlaw had twins Ethan and Natalie.

I end my cancer journey with my mom, Marvel Mae Niebuhr. We took care of her emotionally, physically and medically, and I will cherish it until we meet again. I will be forever grateful to Crossroads Community Hospice. I'm grateful to my family and friends for all pulling together and being a team. I do not feel sorrow. I feel true happiness for this experience that God and Mom have given me. I will always remember her words. "I'm not afraid to die. If I was, I did not know how to live." God bless everyone who goes through the cancer journey with a loved one. The music mom listen to at night time, is now the music I enjoy.

Know the sky is the limit, and you can do anything you set your mind to. I wanted to share my personal experience with hospice with others. Hospice is there to help those who are dying while they are living. Their main goal is to control pain and suffering, not to control death. Some people only have hospice weeks. We had the wonderful experience of seven months.

We turned our cancer journey into something good.

Mom taught us all how to die with courage, dignity, pride and peace. Until we meet again my mom, my hero, and friend, Marvel Mae, I love you! It was a precious gift from God.

Printed in the United States
63142LVS00002B/136-198